Luther

HANS-PETER GROSSHANS

Hans-Peter Grosshans teaches systematic theology and philosophy of religion at the faculty of Evangelical Theology at the University of Tuebingen (Germany), where he is also deputy director of the Institute for Hermeneutics. He studied theology at the universities of Tuebingen and Oxford, and served in the ministry of one of the member churches of the Evangelical Church of Germany for several years. His most recent book is *Theologischer Realismus: Ein sprach-philosophischer Beitrag zu einer theologischen Sprachlehre* (Mohr Verlag, Tuebingen, 1996).

The series editor, Dr Peter Vardy, lectures in Philosophy of Religion at Heythrop College, University of London. He is Course Director of the University of London's External BD programme and a former Chair of the Theology Faculty Board. His other books published by Fount Paperbacks are *The Puzzle of God*, *The Puzzle of Evil*, *The Puzzle of Ethics* and *The Puzzle of the Gospels*, and, most recently, *The Puzzle of Sex*.

PRAISE FOR THE FOUNT CHRISTIAN THINKERS

'This good series of short paperbacks ... are light in weight, but serious in content, giving sketches of major minds in the history of Christian thinking ...

'Dr Vardy paints a vivid portrait of the great Dane Søren Kierkegaard ... Richard Price's expert hands are entrusted with St Augustine ... Paul Rout gives an attractive outline of St Francis and especially of Bonaventure. Sr Anne Murphy writes about Thomas More, crucial in the debate on the early years of the Henrician reformation ... Fr Wilfrid McGreal takes on St John of the Cross and ... helps the reader to grasp his mystical aspirations.

'A surprising but very welcome portrait is of the self-doubting, impassioned Jew Simone Weil ... well written by a Methodist, Stephen Plant.'
HENRY CHADWICK, *THE TABLET*

'These helpfully succinct introductions to the lives and philosophies of their subjects' *TIMES EDUCATIONAL SUPPLEMENT*

'The format makes the subject matter accessible and invites the reader to follow the introduction with further reading from the characters profiled ... in this valuable series.' *CHURCH OF ENGLAND NEWSPAPER*

TITLES IN THE FOUNT CHRISTIAN THINKERS SERIES

AUGUSTINE Richard Price
EVELYN UNDERHILL Ann Loades
FRANCIS & BONAVENTURE Paul Rout
JOHN OF THE CROSS Wilfrid McGreal
KARL RAHNER Karen Kilby
KIERKEGAARD Peter Vardy
LUTHER Hans-Peter Grosshans
SIMONE WEIL Stephen Plant
THOMAS MORE Anne Murphy

LUTHER

Hans-Peter Grosshans

SERIES EDITOR: PETER VARDY

Fount

An Imprint of HarperCollinsPublishers

For Barbara

Fount Paperbacks is an Imprint of
HarperCollins*Religious*
Part of HarperCollins*Publishers*
77–85 Fulham Palace Road, London W6 8JB

First published in 1997 by Fount Paperbacks

1 3 5 7 9 10 8 6 4 2

Hans-Peter Grosshans has asserted the moral right
to be identified as the author of this work

A catalogue record for this book is
available from the British Library

ISBN 0 00 628027 7

Printed and bound in Great Britain by
Caledonian International Book Manufacturing Ltd, Glasgow

Contents

Abbreviations vi

Date Chart vii

Introduction ix

1 Luther's Life 1

2 The Evangelical Experience: The Righteousness of God 13

3 Reforming Christianity 23

4 The Source of Truth: The Word of God 35

5 Faith 55

6 Jesus Christ and Salvation 59

7 The Priesthood of All Believers and the Christian Church 67

8 The Christian Life 73

9 The Concept of Theology 85

Epilogue: Luther's Death 93

Suggested Further Reading 96

Index 99

Abbreviations

The following abbreviations are used in references given in the text:

LW *Luther's Works*. American Edition, ed. by J. Pelikan and H. T. Lehmann, published by Concordia Publishing House (St Louis) and Muhlenberg Press (Philadelphia) in 55 volumes.

WA *Martin Luthers Werke. Kritische Gesamtausgabe* (*Weimarer Ausgabe* = WA), Hermann Böhlaus Nachfolger (Weimar). Not all texts of Luther have been translated into English. Quotations of the WA, which is the main critical edition of Luther's works, are translated by me. In the references to WA, the first number refers to the volume, the second to the page, and the third to the line.

Full bibliographical details of other works cited are given in Suggested Further Reading.

Date Chart

1483	10 November, born in Eisleben
1501	Student of the arts at the university of Erfurt
1505	Master of Arts
	Student of Law
	2 July, thunderstorm and vow
	17 July, enters Augustinian monastery at Erfurt
1507	Ordination to priesthood
	Student of Theology
1508–09	Teaches philosophy at Wittenberg
1510–11	Journey to Rome
1511	Transfer to Wittenberg
1512	Doctor of Theology
	Professor of Biblical Studies
1517	31 October, posting the 95 theses
1518	First interviews and disputations with representatives of the Church
	April, disputation at Heidelberg
	August, the Pope summons Luther to Rome
1519	Leipzig debate between Luther and Eck
1520	Some of the main Reformation writings are published: *On Good Works; The Papacy at Rome; To the Christian Nobility of the German Nation concerning the Reform of the Christian Estate; The Babylonian Captivity of the Church; The Freedom of a Christian*
	October, Luther receives the papal bull

1521	April, Diet of Worms
	4 May, Luther arrives at the Wartburg, where he stays until March 1522
	26 May, edict of Worms: Luther regarded as a convicted heretic and outlawed
	Autumn, evangelical mass with wine to laity; tumult in Wittenberg
1522	Justus Jonas, minister of the Castle Church at Wittenberg, marries
	March, Luther returns to Wittenberg
	September, Luther's German New Testament published
1524	Erasmus, *The Freedom of the Will*
1525	Conflicts with anabaptists and peasants; peasant war
	13 June, Luther and Katherine von Bora marry
	December, *The Bondage of the Will* (against Erasmus)
1526	20 May, birth of first child, John (died 1575)
1527	10 December, birth of daughter Elisabeth (died 3 August 1528)
1528	Publication of the *Confession of the Lord's Supper*
1529	4 May, birth of daughter Magdalena (died 20 September 1542)
	Protest of the princes following the Reformation at the Diet of Speyer
	The Small Catechism; The Large (German) Catechism published
	1–4 October, Marburg colloquy with Zwingli
1530	Diet at Augsburg; presentation of the Augsburg Confession by Philip Melanchthon
1531	9 November, birth of son Martin (died 1565)
1533	28 January, birth of son Paul (died 1593)
1534	Publication of the translation of the complete Bible into German
	17 December, birth of daughter Margarethe (died 1570)
1537	First volume of Luther's German works published
1545	First volume of Luther's Latin works published
1546	23 January, journey to Eisleben
	14 February, Luther's last sermon
	18 February, death in Eisleben

Introduction

Martin Luther was a preacher and teacher who based his theology and his understanding of Christianity on what he considered to be the truth of the Bible. For centuries, he has been highly influential on culture, politics and the Church. He changed the world not by political means but through his words and ideas. Martin Luther had a message which hit a nerve in his time as well as in the hearts and the minds of many of his fellow people. It was this message, in combination with the ideas of fellow reformers like Jean Calvin in Geneva and Huldrych Zwingli in Zürich, which produced those changes in the history of our world we now know as 'the Reformation'.

Luther was a pious man and he had a spiritual message. It was his piety and his spirituality which led him into the monastic life, but it was this same piety and spirituality that led him to criticize the Church and which, later, led him to strip off his monk's habit and to live a civil Christian life.

Luther was a fascinating character and an extremely vital and passionate person. In this book there is only space for a short glance at Luther's biography and some of the main events of his life, before we concentrate on the most important of his ideas and doctrines. Luther's spiritual ideas have had a great and far-reaching influence. The Christian faith was given a new definition by him, and by this faith people were enabled to gain a new understanding of themselves – this new understanding shook the world of his time.

The main critical edition of Luther's works contains more than a hundred volumes, and therefore a short presentation of Luther's theology such as this one will inevitably be fragmentary. However, there is no substitute for reading Luther's main writings or selected works for oneself, and hopefully this volume will encourage such wider reading.

I would like to start by thanking three people without whom this book would not and could not have been written. My thanks are offered to Peter Vardy who has edited it. I am sure he did not realize the extent of the work he would have to do when he asked me, a German, to write a book in his series. His encouragement throughout has been essential, and his criticisms forced me to concentrate on the main ideas of Martin Luther and to present them as clearly as possible. That the whole book may not hurt the eyes of the English-speaking reader is the result of an enormous effort by Anne Vardy, who improved my English in style and grammar. I owe a great debt of gratitude to her. My thanks also to the Revd John Handford, whose excellent knowledge of Luther's theology was of great help and whose comments on the manuscript were pertinent and sharp, but always kindly given.

Luther's Life

Martin Luther was born on 10 November 1483 in the small Saxon town of Eisleben, the son of a miner, Hans Luder, and his wife, Margarethe. He died in the same town on 18 February 1546. Throughout his life, he stayed in his native country: he grew up in Mansfeld, another small town in the kingdom of Saxony; he studied in Erfurt; and he held a chair in theology at the new University of Wittenberg.

Martin Luther was a typical child of his time. It was a time of great change, in which the Middle Ages had reached their end, with major new developments and discoveries in economics, culture, politics and science. Politics was dominated by the Austrian house of Habsburg, in which Charles V (1500–1558) ruled a huge empire that covered central Europe, Spain and the new Spanish colonies in America. It was said that 'the sun did not go down' on his empire. There was a tremendous economic boom and a more pervasive capitalism appeared. Many citizens developed successful smaller companies of their own, and Hans Luder, father of Martin Luther, was an example of this, starting as a miner, but becoming a successful and independent self-employed entrepreneur. Through hard work he became wealthy, and financed the education of his son through both school and university. In the cultural arena, the Renaissance had reached its height, with artists like Michelangelo being sponsored, for example by the popes. With increased wealth and an emerging middle class, education generally became significantly more important, and many new schools and universities were founded, among them the University of Wittenberg (1502).

In these times of tremendous change and such a variety of new activities and innovations, Martin Luther acquired a sound education at school followed by philosophical studies at university. He then – as was his father's wish – began law studies, with the aim of taking up a professional career, and it was as a student of law that he experienced a profound change of heart. One day in July 1505 he was unexpectedly caught in a violent thunderstorm during which he experienced extreme fear and in his anguish made a request and a promise to St Anne, the mother of the Virgin Mary, who was at that time a fairly new and popular saint of the miners: 'St Anne, help me! I will become a monk.' Against strong opposition from his father, Martin, seeing himself bound by his vow, broke off his law studies and, after a farewell party with some friends, entered the Augustinian monastery at Erfurt, which was well known for its ascetic life. Luther chose a life which the Church regarded as the surest way to salvation. The search for a gracious and merciful God was part of the Augustinian understanding of being a monk. When a novice presented himself to an Augustinian congregation the first question the prior asked him was: 'What seekest thou?' And the candidate had to answer: 'God's grace and thy mercy'. Martin Luther entered the monastery in order to make his peace with God and to gain knowledge about God's gracious and merciful will. He spent his days in prayer, in song, in meditation and in quiet companionship. But this peace was shattered by a spiritual experience. His superior selected Luther for the priesthood, and on 2 May 1507 he had to say his first mass. In that mass he experienced the majesty and holiness of God, and this he found terrifying. In the midst of the mass he experienced the terror of the Holy and the horror of the Infinite. The Prior had to persuade him to continue with the mass. What had happened? In the introductory part of the mass Luther had to say: 'We offer unto thee, the living, the true, the eternal God'. Later Luther reported:

At these words I was utterly stupefied and terror-stricken. I thought to myself, 'With what tongue shall I address such Majesty, seeing that all men ought to tremble in the presence of even an earthly prince? Who am I, that I should lift up mine eyes or raise my hands to the divine Majesty? ... At his nod the earth trembles. And shall I, a miserable little pygmy, say "I want this, I ask for that"? For I am dust and ashes and full of sin and I am speaking to the living, eternal and the true God'. (QUOTED IN R. H. BAINTON, *HERE I STAND* 30)

With that experience the possibility of a peaceful and quiet life as a monk faded away. Luther now agonized over the question how he, who was unworthy, could stand before the divine majesty. And how could he, who again always transgressed the divine law in thought, word and deed, confront the divine Holiness? These questions now dominated his spiritual life. Terrified by God's holiness and majesty, his search for God's grace and mercy became more desperate. He experienced trial and desperation. And seldom was he at peace with God. Some years later, however, he had another strong spiritual experience: the experience of the true meaning of the righteousness of God, which opened to him the gates of heaven again (see chapter 2).

Shortly after his first mass, Martin Luther was selected by his superior for the study of theology. In 1510–11, whilst still in the Augustinian monastery in Erfurt, he was sent to Rome where he was for the first time confronted with the very worldly side of the Church. As a pilgrim he walked over the Alps to Italy, but the months in Rome were a shock for Luther. None of his high spiritual expectations were fulfilled. On the contrary he got the impression that in Rome, in the very centre of the Church, there was almost no Christian spirituality. Luther's later attacks against Rome and the Pope were partly the result of this journey.

On his return from Rome in 1511 Luther moved to the Augustinian monastery in Wittenberg, where he became vice-prior in 1512 and later an overseer of other monasteries in the region. After completing his theological studies by gaining his doctorate, he became Professor of Biblical Studies at the University of Wittenberg in 1512, a position he held until his death.

In those years Martin Luther came to know a man who was to be a strong influence on his development, the Vicar General of the Augustinian Order, Johann von Staupitz (1468–1524). In him Luther found his ideal spiritual guide and a strong support for his academic interests as well. Johann von Staupitz, who was fifteen years older than Luther, became almost a second father. Luther could complain to him about all the trials of his faith and his difficulties with Christianity as it was taught by the Church at that time. With this understanding of God and human faith he found that he could gain no certainty about his salvation. He always saw the need to confess his sins and to do penance. Luther agonized with doubt as to whether he was one of the elect destined for life in heaven. Staupitz counselled him, advising him to cling to Jesus Christ and to understand God only through Jesus Christ as recorded in the Bible. It was significant for the development of Luther's theology that Staupitz tried to answer all spiritual and theological questions in this way. Indeed, Luther was to set the Bible and Jesus Christ at the centre of his theology. In later years Luther praised Staupitz as the father of the Reformation, although Staupitz did not follow Luther away from the Catholic Church:

> My good Staupitz said, 'One must keep one's eyes fixed on that man who is called Christ'. Staupitz is the one who started the teaching [of the gospel in our time]. (LW 54, 97)

Luther reported that for the daily readings in the cloister during meals Staupitz wanted only the Bible to be read, and not other spiritual or theological writings and, again, this influenced the young Luther.

When he was appointed to the professorship in biblical studies, Luther had to concentrate on the biblical texts themselves and to develop his theological ideas by interpretation of the Bible. Early signs of Luther's new thinking were already evident in his first lectures. In 1513 he started to lecture on the book of Psalms, in 1515 he lectured on St Paul's Epistle to the Romans, in 1516–1517 he treated the Epistle to the Galatians. In intensive discussion with the theological and philosophical traditions; Luther highlighted the problems there and tried hard to find a new understanding of the Gospel which would meet the needs of his time as well as the turmoil in himself. In those biblical texts he found a new view of God: the holy God, who terrified him, is the All Merciful too. The cross of Jesus Christ shows that there is a reconciliation of God with the world. The God whose holiness and majesty had made Luther feel totally unworthy, had been revealed as a God who deeply loved the world as well.

Beside his duties as professor, Martin Luther was also director of studies, he preached at the castle church of Wittenberg, was an overseer of eleven monasteries, and a parish priest in a village church. It was there that he got to know the disastrous effects on ordinary Christians of the practice of indulgences. People could buy letters of indulgence which were supposed to grant them remission not only from punishment for their sins, but also freedom from their guilt as well.

In 1516 Luther began to criticize this practice in sermons and in academic discussions. In October 1517 he stepped into the limelight with his publication of ninety-five theses which vehemently attacked the ecclesiastical practice of indulgences (see p. 23). The well-known story is that Luther nailed his theses on to the church door at Wittenberg in order to create public interest and discussion. However it is not certain that this did happen. Irrespective of the actual events, however, knowledge and interest in the ninety-five theses spread rapidly across Germany, causing sharp counter-attacks from clerics and lay people. These counter-attacks did not defend the practice of indulgences nor attempt to answer the theses, but tried to accuse Luther of lacking belief. The theses were forwarded by Archbishop Albert of Mainz to Pope Leo X, who first tried to have the problem clarified within the Augustinian Order. This might have been the reason why in 1518 Luther was invited to defend his theology in a disputation before the chapter of the German Augustinians, meeting that year in Heidelberg. But the Augustinians did not want to suppress their brother Martin, who was a true follower of the theology of Augustine (354–430). So it was left to their rivals, the Dominicans, who followed the theology of Thomas Aquinas (1225–1274) which was strongly influenced by the philosophy of Aristotle, to present the case against Luther. In the summer of 1518 the Dominicans succeeded in convincing the Pope to cite Luther to appear in Rome within sixty days to answer charges of heresy. It is important to remember that in those days heretics were normally burnt, and so Luther was in a highly vulnerable position. However, Luther received the assurance of Elector Frederick the Wise, the prince of Saxony, that he would not have to go to Rome, and because of this protection the case against Luther had to be transferred to Germany.

In October 1518 the Pope sent Cardinal Cajetan to interview Luther about his theology and to prove the charges of heresy. The meeting in Augsburg was a disappointment, because Cajetan did not allow Luther to debate the issues, but only gave him an opportunity to recant. When the interview was finished rumour reached Luther that the Cardinal was empowered to arrest him, so by night Luther escaped from Augsburg. His prince, Frederick the Wise, rejected the appeal of Cardinal Cajetan either to banish Luther from his territories or to send him bound to Rome. In the only document he ever sent to Rome on Luther's behalf, Frederick wrote:

As for sending him to Rome or banishing him, that we will do only after he had been convicted of heresy. His offer to debate and submit to the judgement of the universities ought to be considered. He should be shown in what respect he is a heretic and not condemned in advance.
(QUOTED IN R. H. BAINTON, *HERE I STAND* 78)

After this letter, in which Frederick effectively declared Martin Luther his personal protégé, the attacks on Luther moderated. The Roman curia now tried diplomatic means to settle the affair. A series of negotiations and debates followed, culminating in Luther's hearing before the German Diet (or Parliament) in the town of Worms in 1521. However, Rome had already pre-judged the issue without waiting for the hearing, and in the second half of 1520 a papal bull was sent to Luther, declaring that he was a heretic and was excommunicated by the church. The bull also said that all his books should be burnt. Just before he received the papal bull in October 1520 Martin Luther had made a last attempt to come to peace with Pope Leo X. He addressed a diplomatic letter to the Pope expressing great sympathy with him, and with it sent a short treatise on *The Freedom of a Christian*, which he regarded as a summary of his theology. Leo did not react to this letter.

Luther's books were burnt in some cities of Germany in accordance with the papal edict. Fortunately, however, only his books could be burnt. Luther himself remained safe as long as he remained in Saxony, where Frederick could protect him. Luther's excommunication was the beginning of the division in the Church which was to lead to the formation of the new Protestant Churches, and was to influence dramatically the political history of Europe and beyond. As a result of the Reformation the Christian Church was divided into Protestant and Catholic, as well as the Orthodox Church which resulted from the earlier division in 1054.

The new emphasis on German as the national language, the realization that every citizen was a free individual, the importance of individual education and the value of freedom of conscience are ideas that are fundamental to Luther. He has influenced the history of the Western world, because of his unwavering insistence and fight for truth in the cultural, political and religious areas. One of the best-known examples of his determination to hold to his beliefs occurred in 1521, when he appeared before the

German Diet and Emperor Charles V in Worms to defend his position. Luther's refusal to recant in spite of his examination by the German authorities made a marked impression on believers well beyond the boundaries of Germany. In his defence Luther said:

> *Unless I am not convinced by the testimony of the Scriptures or by clear reason (for I do not trust either in the pope or in councils alone, since it is well known that they have often erred and contradicted themselves), I am bound by the Scriptures I have quoted and my conscience is captive to the Word of God.* (LW 32, 112)

He completed his speech in front of the most powerful men of the nation and the emperor Charles V:

> *I cannot and I will not retract anything, since it is neither safe nor right to go against conscience. I cannot do otherwise, here I stand, may God help me. Amen.* (LW 32, 112–13)

In the final edict the majority of the Diet of Worms decided to follow the ecclesiastical lead and to regard Luther as a convicted heretic. He was declared an outlaw. Nobody was allowed to give him further protection. Frederick the Wise, however, decided not to remain loyal to his emperor Charles V and to the German Diet, and he secretly broke the edict of Worms in order to protect and hide Luther. Frederick arranged for him to be kidnapped on the way back from Worms, and secretly Luther was brought to the Wartburg, a castle in Eisenach, where he stayed unrecognized for ten months. Almost nobody knew where he was or even whether he was dead or not. During those months Luther translated the New Testament from its original Greek into German – this was the first time this had been done and was significant as, with the invention of the printing press, the Bible now became available to ordinary people. At the same time many changes were taking place in the

Church all over the country. Luther's friends and followers tried to reform the Church according to his ideas. In Wittenberg the Lord's Supper was now celebrated in a new form by giving wine to the laity. Church liturgy was changed; paintings in churches were destroyed and church music was abolished; monks left their cloisters and the first priests got married. Although still outlawed as a declared heretic, Luther returned to Wittenberg in March 1522, under the protection of Prince Frederick, in order to oversee the reforming process. The Reformers had become more and more radical and had thus begun to threaten the whole process of reformation. Luther's return to Wittenberg was a political signal as well, because it now became obvious that Frederick and other German princes were not obeying the edict of Worms or the Emperor Charles V. Luther had divided the German princes and cities into two: some were loyal to Charles and the Roman Church whilst others protected Luther and began to reform the Church.

There followed very hectic years in which Luther wrote much. He was asked for advice on many and varied matters, and also continued his normal university teaching. He became involved in many conflicts – and the position he took was not always consistent with the teaching of Jesus. For example, when the peasants rebelled in 1525 Luther strongly supported the princes and he justified the butchering of the peasants.

From 1517, academic theological debate began to be increasingly important to him. One example of such disputes occurred in 1524–1525 regarding freedom of will. The debate was between Luther and the most famous scholar at that time, Erasmus of Rotterdam (1467–1536), who was a humanist as well as a moderate Catholic with reforming ideas. Another example was the dispute with his fellow reformer Huldrych Zwingli (1484–1531), which culminated in the Marburg colloquy in 1529 regarding the understanding of the eucharist.

In 1524 Luther left the Augustinian Order and gave up his monastic vows. A year later in 1525, at the age of forty-two, he married the former nun Katherine von Bora (1499–1552), who had asked him to marry her. As a result of Luther's criticism of monastic life, many young monks and nuns had left their monasteries. Katherine was one of these and she had come to Wittenberg, but two years later she was still in domestic service. There were unsuccessful attempts to find her a husband, and in the end she asked Luther if he would not marry her. At first he did not respond seriously to the suggestion but shortly afterwards he agreed. 'I am not infatuated' he was later to say, 'though I cherish my wife.' However he did care for her:

> I would not exchange Katie [as Luther called her] for France or for Venice, because God has given her to me.

With Katherine he experienced the joys and trials of family life alongside his work and writing in church, university and political matters. The family was continually short of money, partly because Luther always had guests at their home but also because Katherine, as a former nun, was without property and Luther's only possessions were his books and clothes. Until his marriage Luther had no personal salary because, according to the statutes of the University of Wittenberg, his monastery had to supply his needs. Once he abandoned the cowl, he was no longer entitled to the revenues of the cloister. After his marriage he was given a regular, though small, salary for his professorship by the new Prince, John. He had no other income, because he refused to take royalties from his books or other writings. In later years the couple acquired a small farm which Katharine managed. Her home-brewed beer was highly praised by her husband. Katherine bore six children, two of whom died young – Elisabeth, aged six months, and Magdalena, aged thirteen, whom Luther loved very deeply. As a family man Luther was more involved in the midst of everyday life than most priests and monks.

The years were filled with theological disputes about doctrinal questions, with the ordering of the new Protestant churches, and with the first moves in the Counter-Reformation – which was the Roman Catholic counter-attack to the Reformation. When Luther died on 18 February 1546, he was by accident in the same town where he had been born, Eisleben. He was there to give advice in some conflicts, when he had a heart attack. He died a few hours later, aged sixty-two.

Luther was not a quiet and diplomatic man. In arguments he liked to use the robust and powerful language of his native countryside. However, despite his abrasive attitude, he was not arrogant and did not claim to be the only person to know the truth. Luther was, rather, a fierce fighter for the truth of the Bible, and it is here that his most important contribution to the Reformation lies. He placed Holy Scripture and its truth at the centre of the life of the Church and of theology. Indeed it is fair to say that Luther did not see himself as a reformer, rather he wanted Scripture to be the reformer of the Church. One of the great disappointments of the Reformation is that the opponents of Luther did not take up his challenge to fight for the truth of the positions they held, but instead resorted to condemnation and the exercise of authority, rather than addressing the issues and the need for reform. This was a missed opportunity as well as a failure to stand up for Luther's vision of a search for truth.

We can now turn to address some of Luther's ideas.

2

The Evangelical Experience:
The Righteousness of God

Martin Luther developed his ideas and religious convictions during and through his interpretation of the Scriptures. He was concerned with the relation of God to human beings and, from this relationship, with human self-understanding. At the heart of Luther's faith and theology is a discussion about the righteousness of God. For Luther it was essential to know how he was to be judged by God after death. In the violent thunderstorm in 1505, he experienced the God who had created him but who also threatened his life as well, and it was this thunderstorm that made him vow to become a monk. When he first said mass in 1507 he experienced the terrifying majesty and holiness of God. In the following years, this sense of the holiness and majesty of God increased. By living a very ascetic monastic life and trying to follow strictly all the monastic rules, Luther tried to become more virtuous. However, he never was satisfied with his spiritual efforts and never had the feeling that he lived up to God's holiness. It was during his study of the Bible that he realized he had misunderstood what God's justice and righteousness meant, and this brought him to a new and deeper understanding.

Luther's realization of the true meaning of God's relationship with human beings has been described as his 'Tower Experience', since it came to him in his study in the tower of the Augustinian monastery in Wittenberg. It was Luther's third major experience of God, and can be called his evangelical experience of the righteousness of God. According to some scholars, Luther had this experience during the first years of his biblical lecturing in 1513–1515, but Luther himself said that this happened in 1519, when he began to interpret the Psalter anew after having lectured on St Paul's epistles to the Romans, Galatians and Hebrews. Luther explained how he had been captivated by an extraordinary desire to understand Paul's Epistle to the Romans. His stumbling block to an understanding of this epistle was the phrase in chapter 1:17, 'In it the righteousness of God is revealed through faith for faith.' In a kind of autobiography written near the end of his life, in 1545, Luther wrote about his 'Tower Experience':

> I hated the words 'righteousness of God' which according to the use and custom of all the teachers I had been taught to understand ... as the ... active righteousness ... with which God is righteous and punishes the unrighteous sinner.

Luther wrestled with this phrase to understand what Paul's true meaning and message was.

> At last, by the mercy of God and meditating day and night, I gave heed to the context of the words, namely 'In it the righteousness of God is revealed, as it is written, "He who through faith is righteous shall live".' There I began to understand that the righteousness of God is that by which the righteous lives by a gift of God, namely by faith and this is the meaning: the righteousness of God is revealed by the Gospel, namely, the passive righteousness with which merciful God justifies us by faith, as it is written, 'He who through faith is righteous shall live.' Here I felt that I was altogether born again and had entered paradise itself through open gates.

The word 'righteousness of God' over which Luther had so agonized and which he had come to dread and hate, became for him the 'sweetest word with a love as great as the hatred with which I had before hated the word' (LW 34, 336–37).

If the righteousness of God was to be understood in the sense of a law, then the just God would be a God who accuses, judges and punishes the human person, and by so doing would be true to the law which demands justice and goodness. Considering the fact that all human beings are sinners and therefore do not live up to the requirements of God, then if God acted justly, this would mean condemnation of all human beings. God would be acting justly in condemning the unjust. This was Luther's understanding prior to the 'tower experience', and it was this that led him to make every possible effort to become a just and holy person. His new theological 'discovery' was that the biblical concept of the righteousness of God was not to be understood by seeing God as a judge, but instead as a truth revealed in the promises of the Gospel. The Gospel promises God's everlasting love and faithfulness to all human beings who have faith. In such a vision of the Gospel the same God who stands against a person as judge and measures the individual according to the commandments of God's law also stands close to the person and supports him or her.

By realizing that God comes close to human beings and accepts them unconditionally, it becomes clear who God is and what his righteousness involves. The righteousness of God does not condemn the unjust, but makes an unjust person righteous. The justification of the nonbeliever and sinner is evident in the words of promise and hope – words like 'Come to me, all who labour and are heavy laden, and I will give you rest' (Matthew 11:28) or 'God so loved the world that he gave his only Son, that whoever believes in him should not perish but have eternal life' (John 3:16). This is not a human but a divine idea of righteousness, which becomes a reality and is valid for all human beings through faith. A person cannot become righteous by his or her own efforts and activities, but is made righteous only by trusting in God's unconditional acceptance and love.

Sin

For Luther Scripture describes:

> ... *man as so turned in on himself that he uses not only physical but even spiritual goods for his own purposes and in all things seeks only himself. This curvedness is now natural for us, a natural wickedness and a natural sinfulness.* (LECTURES ON ROMANS, LW 25, 345)

A person who sees the world only in terms of their own horizons and their own interests is a perfect example of a sinner. For Luther all human beings are sinners, as it is in their natures to care first for themselves. People do not classify themselves as sinners or acknowledge their self-centred way of life as sinful. This suggests that sin is a theological rather than a moral category. Yet God takes the initiative and comes close to us, and exposes human selfishness as an inappropriate way of life. It is through the devotion of God to us that our selfishness is revealed, because we do not devote ourselves totally and unconditionally to other people or to God.

Martin Luther, like Augustine (see Richard Price's book in the 'Fount Christian Thinkers' series on *Augustine* published by HarperCollins in 1996), strongly emphasized human sin. According to Luther, sin is not only a deficiency or shortcoming of a human being or of human nature in general, rather, sin is the explanation for human beings being totally centred on themselves rather than being centred outward. Luther considered human beings to be totally corrupt, to be utterly sinful and to be unable to do any good by their own efforts. This view has led to some seeing Luther as being pessimistic about human nature, with some biographers trying to find psychological reasons in Luther's character to explain this pessimism. However, Luther is not a pessimist. The question should rather be to ask exactly what it is that Luther is pessimistic about and what he means by sin.

For Luther sin is mainly defined as a lack of trust and confidence in God. He uses the concept of sin to give a theological understanding of human beings, which cannot be identified with a wholly pessimistic anthropology. Sin results in humans being unable to relate to and devote themselves to God. Luther says:

> *In all that he does or leaves undone, he rather seeks his own advantage and his own way. He seeks his own honour, rather than God's and that of his neighbour. Therefore, all his works, all his words, all his thoughts, all his life are evil and not godly.* (TREATISE ON GOOD WORKS (1520), LW 44, 72–73)

Human nature

> *... sets for itself no object but itself toward which it is borne and toward which it is directed; it sees, seeks, and works only toward itself in all matters, and it passes by all other things and even God Himself ... as if it did not see them, and is directed only toward itself ... Nature ... sets itself in the place of all other things, even in the place of God, and seeks only those things which are its own and not the things of God. Therefore it is its own first and greatest idol.* (LECTURES ON ROMANS, LW 25, 346)

In this respect even God and faith may be misused, if one follows God's will with selfish motives. People misuse their relation to God, in only relating to God when they hope God might be useful for their own interests and purposes. In this case piety and spirituality are degraded to a mere means to an end, rather than being followed for their own sake. Luther uses the same argument for explaining the morality of a sinner. A person who acts morally may be sinful, if in their moral activities the person is only attempting to satisfy their own interests and purposes, and is not in the first instance interested in the good of fellow human beings alone. Following this general approach Luther notices three characteristics of sin: a sinner is characterized by self-love (*amor sui*), by the desire for security by becoming owner of as many worldly goods as possible (*concupiscentia*), and by an arrogant, haughty self-complacency (*superbia*).

But these are not the only descriptions of sin. We find texts where Luther calls sin the offence against the Ten Commandments. This might occur in two ways: first, if a human being does not fulfil all the commandments; and second – and this is the core of sin – if a human being offends against the first commandment. Human beings are in particular danger of offending against the first commandment in the moral and religious life ('I am the Lord your God ... You shall have no other gods before me'), when they fail to trust and hope in God alone.

For Luther sin is one of the main characteristics of human existence in so far as no human being is able to guarantee permanent trust in God. Sins, therefore, are not only occasional trespasses against the law and will of God in thought, word and deed, but they represent the permanent tendency to trust not in God but in themselves. In one of his sermons Luther concludes: 'Our deficiency does not lie in our works but in our nature' (LW 52, 151). The whole nature of man is characterized by sin. There is nothing else in us but sin: self-love, arrogant self-complacency, and selfish desires go to the very root of what it is to be human.

In piety and morality, for Luther, there lies the danger of the deepest sin, because in trying to be seriously pious and to be seriously moral people are in the deepest sense related only to themselves, and therefore live as if they do not need God in their lives. Luther understood this as being the normal state of human beings but in no way saw this as devaluing humanity. It is the nature of human beings to be related only to themselves, but by indulging in or accepting this nature they are denying their own abilities and possibilities. It is part of the sinful nature of being human that people overestimate themselves. What is more, they do not have the power to change this situation by their own efforts. Luther makes this point when he talks of an enslaved and unfree will of human beings. The will of all humanity is in the last sense related only to humanity itself. Human beings always want – despite their concrete visible activities – to place themselves at the centre and to be concerned for their own welfare. They want to satisfy their own self-love, their own desires and their own complacency.

Some have held the view that people could give up their selfishness by constant practice of love, devotion, humility and chastity. But for Luther it would be a huge self-deception for a person to assume that, by the regular practice of these virtues, he or she will change from being a sinner to becoming holy. On the contrary, this kind of understanding of human salvation is another subtle expression of the hopeless captivity of human beings in sin. Luther is here in opposition to Thomas Aquinas and Aristotle (384–322 BC):

> *Aquinas and Aristotle are wrong when they say that by exercise one becomes virtuous. Like a harpist who becomes a harpist by constant practice, those fools think one can gain the virtues of love, chastity and humility by exercise. It is not true.* (WA 10/3, 92, 19–93, 1)

Human beings can neither set aside their sin nor can they diminish it by exercise of their own will power. Sin is a part of being human and this cannot be separated from human personality. With these ideas as his foundation, Luther argues for a radical position: human beings *are* sinners and they cannot flee this feature of their lives, and as a result of it they are enslaved. Luther radically demythologizes human beings, and their attempts to be something better, nobler and higher are exposed as being self-delusions and illusory.

Nevertheless, at times people do sense that their selfishness and self-centredness is problematic and painful. This happens when they become aware of being trapped in themselves and unable to change and forsake their way of living, thus remaining the same person as before. They are and remain the people they have become. However, they long for liberation from themselves, they long for salvation, for a *new* life, which they cannot gain for themselves because they are trapped. For Luther human beings, especially Christians, are always in this state of tension, feeling trapped by their nature, which dominates their past, and by their selfishness, but at the same time being drawn away from themselves into the future, into freedom, into a new life. They are drawn to other people and to God. This fundamental tension shows that although human beings are sinners, they can develop an awareness of their sin, even an awareness of being completely in the grip of sin.

Justification

Is there any rescue or hope for people who are in such a desperate situation? And where could help and rescue come from? In this situation the righteousness of God becomes important. Normally we would consider it just that people who relate solely to themselves should be left to their own devices. Such people should look to themselves for a way out of their captivity and hopelessness, but by doing this they would merely lead themselves even deeper into their despair.

This is where Luther introduces the righteousness of God. God does not abandon such a person. Because God is love, God is in the first instance interested in a passionate and joyful relationship with each individual, and thinks beyond punishing people for their sins. Righteousness is a concept of relation and refers to the relations of life. God wants the best possible life for each person, and this will come through a relationship between individuals and God. The loving will of God wants each person, as a beloved child of God, to be in relationship with God. It is here that true justice is expressed. It is a justice that human beings have not deserved, but which comes as a free gift from God. Each human being will be judged just by God provided he or she trusts and believes in God's love. People become righteous when, in faith, they turn wholeheartedly to God.

The personal response of faith by each individual is crucial for this message to become effective, because *each individual human being* is at stake when we talk about the righteousness of God. The righteousness of God refers to our lives and to our ongoing relationships. It is not a truth which can be valid and can exist without our involvement. For this reason, it is necessary that each individual should listen, believe and accept God's righteousness if God's justification is to become a reality. Luther's point is not that a person should begin to improve his or her life *in order to* become worthy of God's love and justice – the whole point about God's love is that it is unconditional.

This understanding of God's righteousness and the justification of the godless person is a good example of Luther's rejection of the prevailing theological tradition of his time, and his reinterpretation of key biblical texts. For Luther 'all words take on a new meaning in Christ' (WA 39/2, 94,17f.), because all the words we use in our talk of God have their meaning from their reference to the gracious and loving devotion of God to human beings. Because *God* has come to all people, all can be judged and made righteous and just by God, despite being godless and sinful.

Aristotle said, 'If we act justly, we become just' (*NIKOMACHIAN ETHICS* 1103 b 1f.). Luther disagreed with this: before God people are not just and righteous by virtue of their conduct. This would mean that, by their own efforts, they could make themselves worthy to stand before God's holiness and righteousness. Rather, it is God's love that overcomes human sin and enables every individual to stand before God – nothing can stand in the way of God's love, except an individual's refusal to have faith and to accept this love.

3

Reforming Christianity

The Reformation began with a dispute regarding the understanding of penance and the practice of indulgences in the Church. This provides the best illustration of Luther's understanding of Christian faith.

Luther opened up the issue with ninety-five theses, which he sent on 31 October 1517 to Archbishop Albert of Mainz, and others. He may well have nailed them on to the door of the Castle Church at Wittenberg as well. Prior to this Luther had discussed the problem in academic circles, where his criticisms were even sharper. At stake in the dispute was not merely the practice of indulgences – these were only the visible signs of a more fundamental problem. The real issue was the extent to which Christian faith is directly based on the New Testament.

According to theological understanding in the Middle Ages, a distinction was made between, on the one hand, the permanent, eternal condemnation of a person to hell and, on the other, punishment after death in purgatory for all the sins committed in one's lifetime. The idea was that punishment in purgatory would lead to purification prior to entering eternal life. Eternal damnation could normally be avoided by baptism, in which one became a child of God, but this was not sufficient to secure eternal life. *Original sin*, which since Adam's fall was an essential characteristic of human existence, could not prevent the achievement of future eternal bliss by the baptized, but it still retained its power and had not been totally nullified. Original sin was still effective and ever present. The *actual sins* of human beings could not be overlooked, but had to be confessed and punished by God in order to restore goodness to the sinners. This took place in purgatory which cleansed and punished the sinner for his or her sins. Through their suffering in purgatory, human beings were prepared for an eternal blessed life in the presence of God.

Through penance in this life people could try to avoid punishment in purgatory and could serve a part of their punishment here. Penance was the central doctrine by which human beings were justified and by which people related to God. Through penance people could take on some punishment for their sins and cleanse their lives in order to restore their goodness and to secure eternal life. The Church claimed to know the appropriate penance for each sin, and each believer told the priest, in confession, details of the sin he or she had committed. The Church claimed the power to be able to forgive sins, to restore people to a right relation with God, and to secure their eternal life. The Church was the holder of the 'office of keys' (the keys to open or close paradise), which were conferred upon the Church by Christ (Matthew 16:19). This office of keys had the power of liberating people from their captivity by forgiving them their sins and opening paradise for them. One way to do penance for sin was to buy a letter of indulgence.

Indulgences were a means used by the Church to enable people to escape some of the punishment for their sins which would otherwise have occurred in purgatory after death. To secure indulgences, people, beside certain spiritual penances, had to pay sums of money which would secure their release from punishment in purgatory. This gave rise to the well-known rhyme:

As soon as the coin in the coffer rings,
The soul from purgatory springs.

The attractions to a person of paying substantial sums to the Church to secure release from punishment in purgatory were very great, and the Church derived a very considerable income from the sale of indulgences.

Initially Luther did not reject the idea of purgatory as a place of punishment and cleansing after death, but finally he came to reject the whole idea. From 1530 on he accepted only the alternatives of heaven and hell. Prior to this, in 1517, it was the practice of indulgences which represented the central focus for his attack. Indulgences were used not only to save souls, but also to satisfy the enormous financial needs of the Church.

Luther knew only part of the financial and political background to the practice of indulgences in Germany. Pope Leo X had granted Albert of Brandenburg, who was in desperate need of money, the privilege of dispensing indulgences in his territories. Albert, who was then Bishop of Magdeburg and Halberstadt, was successful in obtaining the archbishopric of Mainz as well, which made him both the spiritual and also the political primate of Germany. For this irregularity of holding three bishoprics at once he had to pay high fines both to the Pope and to the Emperor. He was forced to take out a huge loan from Fugger's bank, and soon needed even more money to pay the interest. Pope Leo X arranged with Albert that half of the returns from indulgences, in addition to the fine Albert had already paid, should go to him to help meet the cost of building the new church of St Peter's in Rome. Albert was allowed to use the remaining half to reimburse his bankers.

However, it was not this financial and political background which provoked Luther's primary criticism but the spiritual and theological problems to which it gave rise. Luther saw the disastrous effects – both materially and psychologically – of the practice of indulgences in his pastoral work amongst ordinary people. His concern was, as he wrote to Albert in the covering letter to his ninety-five theses: 'that the people may learn the Gospel and the love of Christ' (WA Br 1, No. 48, 40–41).

At the heart of Luther's view in his ninety-five theses was his radical new understanding of penance, which derives solely from the New Testament. In his first thesis he wrote:

> *When our Lord and Master Jesus Christ said, 'Repent' [Matthew 4:17], he willed the entire life of believers to be one of repentance.'*
> (LW 31, 25)

The emphasis lies on 'the entire life' of the individual, which means that penance cannot be practised merely once or even occasionally. Repentance

> *... cannot be understood as referring to the sacrament of penance, that is, confession and satisfaction, as administered by the clergy.*
> (THESES 2, LW 31, 25)

One cannot delegate one's own relation to God to the mediation of priests between human beings and God. Luther has a new understanding of penance, which he now uses in the sense of repentance. For Luther this sense is shown in Mark's gospel 1:15, in which, in its Latin version, Jesus was talking about penance. However in the original Greek text Jesus was saying '*Repent* and believe!' The word for repentance in the original Greek New Testament literally means 'change your mind'. This shift in meaning enabled Luther to give the doctrine of penance a new definition. It is only through a change of mind and a turn to God – not through doing penance – that people can clarify their relation to God, have their goodness restored and thus secure eternal life.

Luther considered that the Church's use of indulgences separated apparent penance from genuine faith and trust in God. Penance became an autonomous instrument of the Church. If the practice of the Church dispensing indulgences were to be accepted, Luther maintained that a person no longer had the possibility of a direct relationship with God. In his thirty-sixth thesis he wrote:

Any truly repentant Christian has a right to full remission of penalty and guilt, without the need for letters of indulgence. (LW 31, 28)

Anyone who has repented of his or her sins and deeply regrets having turned away from God has, Luther considered, already turned back to God by the very act of repentance and regret. This action alone is sufficient for God to forgive all.

As set out earlier (p. 7), in 1520 Luther wrote a diplomatic letter to Pope Leo X trying to come to a peaceful reconciliation with him and to avoid excommunication. With this letter he sent one of his most important essays, *The Freedom of a Christian*, calling it 'a small book if you regard its size. Unless I am mistaken, however, it contains the whole of Christian life in a brief form, provided you grasp its meaning' (LW 31, 343). In that essay Luther wrote about faith:

When, however, God sees that we consider him truthful and by faith of our heart pay him the great honour which is due him, he does us that great honour of considering us truthful and righteous for the sake of our faith. Faith works truth and righteousness by giving God what belongs to him. Therefore in turn God glorifies our righteousness.
(LW 31, 351)

Luther rejected the official Church's claim that she administers the merits of Christ and the saints like some sort of treasure, which she can distribute to believers and, by doing so, can compensate for their sins:

Nor are they [viz. the indulgences] the merits of Christ and the saints, for, even without the Pope, the latter always work grace for the inner man, and the cross, death, and hell for the outer man. (LW 31, 30)

Rather 'the true treasure of the Church is the most holy Gospel of the glory and grace of God' (LW 31, 31). It is the Gospel which promises the godless and sinful human being the forgiveness of sins. The Gospel is a treasure which is 'naturally most odious, for it makes the first to be last' (LW 31, 31).

The significance of Luther's theses was that he not only criticized the misuse of indulgences, but also questioned the whole theological basis on which this practice was founded. Luther was surprised at the vehement nature of the counter-attack from the Church, and was particularly saddened that the Church charged him with heresy rather than taking up the theological issues he had raised. He quickly came to realize the dangers of holding his own position, because heretics were not only threatened by the Church, but the civil authorities were faithful servants of the ecclesiastical judiciary who would punish the heretic. Luther's opponents compared him with the Czech Jan Hus (1369–1415), who was burnt in 1415 for heresy. When in 1520 Luther was declared a heretic by Pope Leo X, he was threatened with the same fate as Jan Hus.

Luther reacted immediately to the attack on him, and repeatedly specified his own understanding of penance and faith. In his *Explanations of the Ninety-Five Theses or Explanations of the Disputation concerning the value of Indulgences* (1518), Luther came to the conclusion that:

> *The Church needs a reformation which is not the work of one man, namely the Pope, or of many men, namely the Cardinals ... but it is the work of the whole world, indeed it is the work of God alone. However, only God who has created time knows the time for this reformation. In the meantime we cannot deny such manifest wrongs. The power of the keys is abused and enslaved to greed and ambition.* (LW 31, 250)

Luther now called for more rigorous limitations to papal power. He also formulated his ideas of faith more clearly:

We are justified by faith, and by faith also we receive peace, not by works, penance, or confessions. (LW 31, 105)

This does not mean, however, that Luther rejected the need for the Pope or for priests – indeed he praised them both. His attitude to the Pope and priests is a good example of Holy Scripture being the exclusive basis for Luther's theological thinking. According to the New Testament, Jesus said to St Peter:

I will give you the keys of the kingdom of heaven, and whatever you bind on earth shall be bound in heaven, and whatever you loose on earth shall be loosed in heaven. (MATTHEW 16:19)

Luther accepted that the keys of heaven were conferred upon Peter, and with that upon the Church. But Luther restricted his understanding of the range of the office of keys by his interpretation of Matthew 16:19, which says: 'whatever you loose *on earth ...*', which means that the office of keys does not extend to heaven, and the Church cannot loose people in purgatory – yet this is what was promised by the letters of indulgence. The Church's power is confined to this world – and her power of keys is necessary to liberate and redeem people and to save and heal their lives.

The process of liberation and salvation of individuals was described by Luther in his explanation to thesis 7:

When God begins to justify a man, he first of all condemns him; he whom he wishes to raise up, he destroys. (LW 31, 99)

It is characteristic of Luther's theology that the negative side of the relationship with God, that is, the remoteness of God and the consciousness of oneself as being lost, is understood as being caused by God. It is God who leads people into the despair which is found when one becomes locked into a relationship with oneself. In

Luther's first hymn 'Dear Christians, let us now Rejoice' (1523) he sets out the position:

> *I fell but deeper for my strife,*
> *there was no good in all my life,*
> *for sin had all possessed me.* (LW 53, 219)

Luther says with Samuel, the prophet:

> *The Lord kills and makes alive, he leads to hell and leads out again.*
> (1 SAMUEL 2:6)

God leads people to hell, that is, into a situation which is characterized by total ungodliness and in which people have to exist merely related to themselves. However, God does not lead people to hell and with that into the despair about their own lost and lonely existence in order to leave them there, but to lead them out again into true life.

> *Here ... God works a strange work in order that he may work his own*
> *work. This is true contrition of heart and humility of spirit, the sacri-*
> *fice most pleasing to God.* (LW 31, 99)

People who come to despair and rely entirely on themselves cannot perceive anything of a merciful and justifying God, but instead have the impression of their own damnation being near. If they relate their situation to God, they will feel that their despair is due to God's wrath. However, for Luther it is in the very experience of losing oneself before God, that the grace of God is already present. This negative experience of one's own life is actually caused by God's grace and mercy. Luther considered that it is a requirement for real devotion to God that human beings first have to see themselves as locked into a relationship with themselves, and thereby to become conscious of being lost. This requirement is necessary in order for the individual to come to be able to turn their eyes away from themselves. Through despair, they learn to expect everything from God.

The Church comes into the process of healing, liberation and salvation through the priest:

> *When the priest sees such humility and anguish, he shall, with complete confidence in the power given him to show compassion, loose the penitent and declare him loosed, and thereby give peace to his conscience.* (LW 31, 100)

Luther considered that Jesus Christ gave the priestly office great importance, yet the effectiveness of the grace of God does not come from the priestly or ecclesiastical action, but from God. The grace of God is hidden: 'The remission of guilt takes place through the infusion of grace before the remission by the priest' (LW 31, 101). Because the grace of God is hidden, human beings are not conscious of the graciousness and loving devotion of God, even though it has already been given. Because grace is invisible:

> *... as a general rule we are not sure of the remission of guilt, except through the judgement of the priest ... Moreover, as long as we are uncertain, there is no remission, since there is not yet remission for us.* (LW 31, 101)

The priest is important in the whole process of salvation, but is clearly secondary to the gracious divine action which results in the remission of sin. Luther rejects the view 'that God does not remit guilt unless there is a prior remission by the priest' (LW 31, 98), and in so doing challenges the theological position of the priest in the process of salvation. This is one of Luther's central arguments against the traditional definition of the priest, and against the position of the Pope's claimed authority as the 'bearer of the keys'.

Luther's criticism of the Pope developed further, and came to a peak in 1520 when, in an essay 'On the Papacy in Rome', he claimed that the papacy was not founded by Christ. Instead he claimed that Christ had not given the keys of heaven to St Peter alone but to the whole Christian community – from which follows the idea of the priesthood of all believers.

A false understanding of the grace of God and of the Christian faith is one in which:

> *people learn to trust in the delusion that it is possible to have their sins cancelled by their contritions and satisfactions.* (LW 31, 103)

For Luther it is this understanding that gives rise to the belief in justification by works, that is, the attempt to enter into a relationship with God through one's own efforts. Any such religious efforts are expressions of total sin.

In 1518 – while Luther was still an Augustinian monk – the chapter of the German Augustinians met in Heidelberg. Luther was invited to discuss his new approach to theology with them. At that time many Augustinian monks were sympathetic to Luther's ideas, for he was well known and highly respected. Most of them disliked the polemic attacks against Luther by church officials, and wanted to show him their sympathy by providing the opportunity for a theological discussion of his ideas. In the *Heidelberg Disputation* Luther claimed:

> *The person who believes that he can obtain grace by doing what is in him adds sin to sin so that he becomes doubly guilty.* (LW 31, 50)

Penance and actions intended to obtain divine grace and God's remission of sins are not the starting point of faith, but are the results of the grace of God. As a consequence of the experience of God revealing one's misery, an individual may turn their life once again towards God and God's will. Repentance represents the turn to a new way of living life in harmony with God. This mission will not end on earth as long as one lives. Therefore the whole life of a Christian should be repentance, because it is characterized by the task of relating one's life to the loving God by constant critical self-correction.

Luther's doctrine of justification by faith does not imply that people can gain salvation without any effort. His approach is full of the dynamism of the experience of the grace of God. God does everything for his beloved people, and we can relate to God only when we let God do everything for us, and when we expect and hope for everything we need from God. We can do nothing for our own salvation other than to trust totally in God's love and righteousness. Faith should, therefore, be a joyous experience. It is because of the experience of faith that a person becomes eager to make efforts towards a new life. This creates the desire to bring one's life into correspondence with God's will.

To Luther, it is obvious that a loving relationship with God can only be achieved by each individual, and that this relationship has radical consequences for each person's own life, just as love has direct consequences for the lives of lovers. The starting point, however, for the love relationship between God and human beings is God's unconditional love, and this is what Luther means by grace. Because individuals become aware of God's love, they wish to improve their lives to please their partner and their lover – God.

Luther conceived God not as the highest principle or first cause. For Luther, God, the creator of the world and of all life, was above all a personal God. Therefore Luther claimed he could talk with God in the same way as with other people, and he stressed in his writings this personal quality of the relationship to God. It is part of this relationship that the word of God, contained in the Bible, is given to us.

4

The Source of Truth: The Word of God

Luther's own description of his 'tower experience' showed that he gained his insights from the study of the Bible and his persistent struggle to make its meaning plain. He is, however, in no way a biblical fundamentalist. He claims that the Bible can be the source and norm for human knowledge of God, but that this does not mean that the biblical texts are literally dictated by God to their authors. God speaks to human beings through the words of the Bible and, when this happens, the texts become the word of God. Every sermon is an opportunity for the word of God to be made known, and this may happen in other situations in life as well. God is present in the world through God's word – and it is this subject that interests Luther as a theologian.

In describing Luther's doctrine of the word of God it is necessary to go through three stages:

To clarify Luther's understanding of the Bible and its relation to the word of God;

To consider how Luther relates reason to the Bible; and

To discuss what God actually has to say to people in the law and the Gospel.

The Bible

At the time Luther was writing, the new printing technology invented by Johann Gutenberg (1400–1467), using movable, metal letters, had become widespread, and with it a new stage in human history began, facilitated by ease of communication. Before this invention people communicated mostly by word of mouth, but the new printing methods were used to spread Luther's ideas. The main benefit to Luther of the new printing methods was that the Bible could now be read by lay people, and through this believers could free themselves from the theologians and priests who had previously been the only mediators of God's word.

In 1516 the leading scholar of his time, Erasmus of Rotterdam, had edited the first Greek edition of the New Testament, called *Novum instrumentum*, and this greatly assisted Luther in his task. Erasmus was a humanist (for further explanations of the term 'humanist', which has a different meaning from that used today, see chapter 2 of Anne Murphy's book on *Thomas More* in the 'Fount Christian Thinkers' series), who wanted to reform the Church and renew Christianity, particularly in the light of the Sermon on the Mount (Matthew 5–7). The central motto of the humanist movement was '*ad fontes*' – that is, 'back to the original sources of human experience and knowledge'. These sources were the classical Greek and Latin texts as well as the original Greek and Hebrew texts of the Bible. Humanists like Erasmus were convinced that Christianity could be renewed only by returning to its roots. Luther shared this conviction. When in 1518 the humanist Philipp Melanchthon (1497–1560) arrived in Wittenberg as the new professor of Greek, Luther quickly got in touch with him. Melanchthon, although only twenty-one when he came to Wittenberg, already enjoyed a European reputation as a learned humanist. He had no commitment to Luther on his arrival, but soon converted to Luther's position, because he agreed with Luther's interpretation of the apostle Paul. Luther and Melanchthon became close friends, and Melanchthon became, after Luther, the most important leader of the Reformation.

Luther was following the humanist's 'back to the roots' motto when he first translated the New Testament from the original Greek into German in 1521. Later, he, with other scholars like his friend Melanchthon, translated the Old Testament from Hebrew into German. This was difficult because, at the time, there was no single uniform German language. It was Luther who, with his translation of the Bible, created the German language as it is used today. It is interesting to note, however, that he thought that the preaching or telling of the word of God was better done orally than in writing. For Luther the Gospel was fundamentally an oral message and was best transmitted through sermons:

> Christ did not write his doctrine himself ... but transmitted it orally, and also commanded that it should be orally continued giving no command that it should be written. (LW 52, 205)

> So it is not at all in keeping with the New Testament to write books on Christian doctrine. Rather in all places there should be fine, goodly, learned, spiritual, diligent preachers without books, who extract the living word from the old Scripture and unceasingly inculcate it into the people, just as the apostles did. For before they wrote, they first of all preached to the people by word of mouth and converted them ... However, the need to write books was a serious decline and a lack of the Spirit which necessity forced upon us ... For when heretics, false teachers, and all manner of errors arose in the place of pious preachers ... then every last thing that could and needed to be done, had to be attempted ... So they began to write in order to lead the flock of Christ as much as possible by Scripture into Scripture. They wanted to ensure that the sheep could feed themselves and hence protect themselves against the wolves, if their shepherds failed to feed them or were in danger of becoming wolves too. (LW 52, 206)

The picture of the sheep which become their own shepherds shows the emancipatory effect of Luther's translation. But Luther did not simply identify the Bible with the word of God. He distinguished between the Bible as a book which represents the Holy Scripture of the Christian Church, and the word of God which represents those parts of the Bible used to address people directly, for example in sermons or in pastoral care. Of course there is a close connection:

> *No book may comfort except the Holy Scripture ... because it contains the word of God.* (WA 10, 75,3-7)

Luther did not understand the biblical texts as being the absolute truth, but in each case when he read texts of the Bible questioned whether they proclaimed Christ crucified and risen from the dead for the salvation of all people, as well as the doctrine of justification by faith alone. This he regarded as the Bible's own internal measure of truth, which makes it possible to criticize the biblical texts. Luther claims that Christ is the only content of Scripture: 'Without doubt the whole Scripture is orientated to Christ alone' (WA 10/2, 73, 15). With this as the criterion for judging the truth of biblical texts, Luther radically criticizes whole books of the Bible. In his judgement, the Letter of James, the Letter to the Hebrews and the book of the Revelation to John do not belong amongst the main books of the New Testament, because these texts are not orientated to Christ alone. Nevertheless, because of his respect for tradition and its selection of the biblical canon, Luther did not eliminate those Scriptures from his German Bible. He did, however, alter the sequence of the Scriptures in the New Testament, and put those three texts at the end of the Bible.

For Luther, Holy Scripture was the only source and norm for any knowledge of God. Having said this, he used the texts critically and without accepting them blindly. However, the text was not judged against external criteria but by the context of the Bible as a whole. Luther claimed:

Christ is the Lord, not the servant, the Lord of the Sabbath, of law and of all things. The Scriptures must be understood in favour of Christ, not against him. For that reason they must either refer to him or must not be held to be true Scriptures. (LW 34, 112)

Luther further developed his understanding of Scripture in discussion with the traditional Catholic understanding, with the anabaptist movement which became especially strong in 1525, and in his reply to Erasmus of Rotterdam, in *The Bondage of the Will* (to which we will return later, see p. 43).

The discussions were about the authority of Scripture and who guarantees its truth. Early in his disputes with the authorities of the Church, Luther had used the authority of Scripture against some of her doctrines and practices. The Church's official claim was that the Church, which had combined the different biblical texts to create the canon of the New Testament, is the guarantor of the authority of Scripture. Luther, however, did not agree to this subordination of Scripture to the Church and her tradition. Instead he maintained the principle that Scripture was self-authenticating: Scripture has and needs no guarantor other than itself. By this Luther did not mean that the Bible itself was inspired by God simply because it says so (for instance, the second letter of St Paul to Timothy (3:16) says: 'All Scripture is inspired by God'). Such a circular argument was far too weak. Luther rather held a realist position: the authority of Holy Scripture is wholly founded on its contents which refer to Jesus Christ and the divine process of human salvation. Therefore the authority of Scripture *depends on the truth of its central contents*, which are about the relation of God to human beings – nobody and nothing else could give Scripture authority, not even an institution like the Church. Here again we see Luther's stress on truth. The Bible is not true simply because it says so – what makes the Bible true is that it truthfully records God's work of salvation.

Therefore the authority of Scripture and its binding nature upon those who believe in it depends not on the fact that the

Church as a community of people has selected and combined the biblical books together to form the Christian canon – rather church authority depends on the truth of Scripture.

There follows an obvious consequence from this position. The true meaning of the biblical texts is to be found in their reference to the loving and just God and God's gracious relation to human beings, which for Luther is the same as the referring to Jesus Christ. All former and present interpretations of the biblical texts have to be evaluated in this light. Luther sums up this position by saying that Scripture interprets itself. Scripture is:

> *totally certain ... quite easy to understand, completely revealed, its own interpreter.* (WA 7, 97, 23)

> *Therefore Scripture is its own light. It is splendid when Scripture interprets itself.* (WA 10/3, 238, 10)

This principle is used by Luther against the traditional position which held that the teaching office of the Church, guided by the Holy Spirit, has the authority and competence to give a true interpretation of Scripture.

Luther also opposed the understanding of Scripture put forward by the new anabaptist movements. To explain this we first have to consider their origins. As a result of Luther's reforming thoughts some of his followers developed even more radical ideas. In 1521–1522 Luther had to be kept hidden in the Wartburg because he was threatened with death after his excommunication, and could not return to Wittenberg. Some of his friends and followers introduced radical changes in the parish of Wittenberg.

One of these, Andrew Carlstadt (1480–1541), was one of the inspirational figures for the 'radical wing' of the Reformation. In 1522 Carlstadt and others introduced reforms such as the marriage of priests and the rejection of divine orders. They also destroyed all paintings in the churches and abolished church music, because the divine Spirit was considered able to dispense with all external aids, whether of art or music. Luther did not agree with all of those reforms. In particular, he himself loved church music and thought it had an important place in worship, to which he contributed many hymns of his own composition.

Another prominent figure of the 'radical wing' of the Reformation was Thomas Müntzer. Ordinary people expected that, with the coming of the Reformation, their conditions of life would now improve. 'Prophets' like Müntzer preached the end of the world. In 1525 he proclaimed that the kingdom of God was at hand, and he fomented a rebellion of peasants in Saxony. In fact, all over Germany the peasants rebelled, but their rebellions were crushed by the armies of the princes. Müntzer himself was caught and beheaded.

Luther's role in those conflicts in 1525 was very ambiguous, and on the whole it is a part of his life which does him no credit. Although Carlstadt and Müntzer, and the peasants as well, had been inspired by Luther's ideas, for Luther they were far too radical and they threatened the success of the Reformation. He therefore first acquiesced in the banishment of his former friend, Carlstadt, from Saxony. Carlstadt departed, claiming in the same words that Luther had used after the Diet of Worms that he had been condemned 'unheard and unconvicted' and that he had been expelled by his former colleague. Carlstadt went to the south of Germany, where he gained support for his ideas and was given a teaching post, first in Zürich and then in Basle.

In addition, Luther actively assisted the German princes to put down the peasants and the radical Christians who sided with them. In 1525 he wrote two essays, 'Against the Heavenly Prophets' and 'Against the Robbing and Murdering Hordes', which were the starting signal for the princes and their armies to crush the peasants and radical Christians. This they did with great bloodshed and they appealed to Luther's writings for justification.

Because of these actions, many ordinary people were no longer enthusiastic about Luther and his reforming ideas. However,

Luther's support for the princes had pragmatic benefits as he gained the support of many of them to reform the Church in their countries in accordance with his ideas.

The 'radical wing' of the Reformation was termed an anabaptist movement because they rejected infant baptism and considered that each adult had to be baptized again. They stressed the inward and spiritual side of Christian life, and the Holy Spirit was set in opposition to the letter of Scripture. Being possessed by the Holy Spirit was made the necessary qualification for church membership. Within their religious communities leadership fell to the spirit-filled, be they clergy or lay. Quite often the result was the abolition of a professional ministry. Müntzer clearly expressed this concentration on the divine spirit:

> God does disclose himself in the inner word in the abyss of the soul. The man who has not received the living witness of God really knows nothing about God, though he may have swallowed a hundred thousand Bibles. God comes in dreams to his beloved as he did to the patriarchs, prophets, and apostles ... God pours out his Spirit upon all flesh, and now the Spirit reveals to the elect a mighty and irresistible reformation to come. (QUOTED IN R. H. BAINTON, HERE I STAND 204)

Anabaptists claimed that a true interpretation of the biblical texts needed a special spiritual talent, which is a gift from God to particular people. Luther did not ignore the significance of the Holy Spirit for the interpretation of Scripture, but he considered that the spirit in which people are able to give a true interpretation of the Bible has to be the spirit of Scripture itself.

For Luther the Catholics and the anabaptists were both 'enthusiasts', because in their interpretations they subjugated Scripture under external rules. It is for this reason that Luther was suspicious of an allegorical, pictorial interpretation of the biblical texts, and instead emphasized the view that they should be interpreted in a simple, literal sense. Luther assumes this to be possible in most cases, because he considers the Bible to be clear in itself, and its stories have simple meanings which follow from their essential content, which is Jesus Christ.

In 1525, the same year in which Luther was involved in conflicts with the anabaptists and the peasants, he wrote an extensive essay *The Bondage of the Will*, answering a substantial critique of his theological ideas by Erasmus which had been published a year before. Erasmus was a moderate Catholic and, as we have seen, a humanist, but was also a critic of the Church and saw its great abuse being in the externalization of religion. Erasmus was the most famous scholar of his time, and was urged by prominent persons, for example King Henry VIII of England, to declare his position concerning Luther. He did this in a tract entitled *The Freedom of the Will*, in which he did not oppose Luther's position on the papacy and indulgences etc., but Luther's anthropology. The tract went 'to the heart of the problem', as Luther recognized, and it took him over a year to answer it. A fundamental part of Luther's *The Bondage of the Will* is about the understanding of Scripture, and it is here that Luther introduced a new distinction between an external and an internal clarity of Scripture.

> *To put it briefly, there are two kinds of clarity in Scripture, just as there are also two kinds of obscurity: one external and pertaining to the ministry of the Word, the other located in the understanding of the heart. If you speak of internal clarity, no man perceives one iota of what is in the Scriptures unless he has the Spirit of God. All men have a darkened heart, so that even if they can recite everything in Scripture ... yet they apprehend and truly understand nothing of it ... For the Spirit is required for the understanding of Scripture ... If, on the other hand, you speak of the external clarity, nothing at all is left obscure or ambiguous.* (LW 33, 28)

Erasmus had claimed that Scripture contains obscure parts which make it necessary to have their interpretation decided by the church authorities. Against that position Luther argued that Scripture is clear in itself, and therefore it is not necessary for the church authorities to give an authoritative interpretation. In rejecting the need for the authority of the Church, Luther defended the freedom and rationality of the individual Christian far more than did Erasmus.

Human Reason

In the light of the high significance ascribed to Scripture both for human knowledge of God and for the salvific relation of God to human beings, the question has to be raised of how Luther judged human reason and how he saw the relationship between reason and the Bible.

Luther's view of human reason is both positive and negative. His negative view is based on the conflict between Scripture and reason. Reason is part of the whole human person who, as a sinner, wants to exist and act by him- or herself. Scripture competes with reason, because being external to human beings it wants to say something to them which demands their acknowledgement and response. It is in this sense that, in 1528, Luther explained the third article of the apostolic creed in his *Small Catechism*:

I believe that I cannot by my own understanding or effort believe in Jesus Christ my Lord or come to him. (WHAT DOES THIS MEAN? 120)

Sinners, as rational beings, want to develop knowledge and convictions by themselves and do not want to have them imposed. At this point Luther began his criticism of reason, which in its self-relatedness and its absolute will to self-determination does not want to hear about its own good from somebody else, and does not want to acknowledge such an external good. Luther vehemently decried such reason. In one of his strongest attacks, Luther described reason as 'the best whore the devil has' (WA 51, 126, 9f.). The post-Enlightenment view of the second half of the nineteenth and of the twentieth century was to return to Luther's position and to use his polemics and critique of human reason to challenge the Enlightenment, which had given first priority to reason. In this sense Luther lays down a challenge to Kantian ways of thinking which see reason as supreme. Søren Kierkegaard followed in Luther's footsteps in this respect (see the *Kierkegaard* volume in the 'Fount Christian Thinkers' series by Peter Vardy).

The Lutheran theological tradition continued this kind of criticism and condemnation of reason, but Luther's positive attitude towards reason was overlooked. A good example can be found in his disputation 'Concerning Man' in 1536, in which he put forward a strong case in favour of reason. Reason, he says, is a gift from God. Again in his *Small Catechism*, in the explanation to the first article of the apostolic creed, Luther says:

> *I believe that God has created me and all other creatures, and has given me, and preserves for me, body and soul, eyes, ears, and all my limbs, my reason and all my senses.* (WHAT DOES THIS MEAN? 114)

With God's gift of reason, human beings are able to realize their task of dominion over creation (Genesis 1:28). Culture, art and science, medicine and law are created and preserved by reason. Reason is:

> *the inventor and mentor of all the arts, medicines, laws and of whatever wisdom, power, virtue, and glory men possess in this life.*
> (THE DISPUTATION CONCERNING MAN, LW 34, 137)

All these achievements of reason should not be ignored but, on the contrary, should be highly respected and praised. Luther welcomed all the new activity in the sciences of his time. Those tasks awarded majesty to reason and showed its divine origin:

And it is certainly true that reason is the most important and the highest ranking among all things and, in comparison with other things in this life, the best and something divine. (LW 34, 137)

It is true that the tasks given to reason are strictly related to this earthly life, but reason should develop and order the earthly life of man. Reason 'is a sun and a kind of god appointed to administer these things in this life' (LW 34, 137). In this area reason is the court of last appeal. Reason has the competence to decide the best arrangements for economics and politics. Theology and Scripture, on the other hand, do not produce political or economic doctrines, but they respect reason's ability to handle earthly affairs.

It is important to note that Luther did not consider the competence of reason to have been lost as a result of Adam's fall. Godless people are able, with their reason, which was given to them by God, to organize and develop all earthly affairs well:

Nor did God after the fall of Adam take away this majesty of reason, but rather confirmed it. (LW 34, 137)

Reason has lost its way, because after Adam's fall, it no longer recognizes its own majesty and dignity. Reason has become independent from its source (God) and now claims to be able to take responsibility *for the whole* of a person's life. Thus reason has chosen to go beyond its own limitations and possibilities.

For Luther, reason's rebellion against God has at least two results. The first is that reason becomes high-handed: human beings praise themselves because of what they see reason as having achieved. These achievements are no longer understood as stemming from God, but as being due solely to human ability. The second result is that human beings who live without God misuse reason. Reason is no longer set in the context of the task God has given to mankind, but is used simply to look after individual human interests. Reason's rebellion shows that it is blind to the truth, that it is corrupt, and that it is in itself not able to see the truth about itself. It is true that reason in a certain sense has the ability to know God – especially to know the *existence* of God – but reason is so strongly related to earthly affairs, that it is not possible for it truly to come to know God. Moreover, to reason the word of God and faith in God seem to be a closed book.

Reason therefore needs faith to see itself in its proper context, and it needs to be put into a true relationship with God. If this happens reason becomes an excellent and invaluable tool of faith, for example in being used to interpret biblical texts.

For Luther, the perversion and misuse of reason was obvious in people's attempts to get to know God on their own. People who do not want to orientate their lives to God have to be responsible for their own lives, and they use reason to develop and justify their own ideas of what is good and what is evil. Necessarily this produces a moralistic and self-righteous attitude in life. Reason not only tries to develop and justify its own standard of what a good life is, but also attempts to control its realization as well. Therefore reason will always find arguments to justify a person's living on their own terms. Normally, reason will cling to its own ideas of what is good and what is evil, and thereby will judge its own life as good. This is self-righteousness and for Luther this is the greatest sin. Such a person is solely related to him- or herself and thereby radically ignores and avoids God.

Not everyone is on the right path merely because they are 'religious'. God may well be completely ignored and a human idea of religion substituted. Luther emphasized knowing God truly, and not merely as a principle to satisfy moral and self-righteous inclinations. He believed that many people understood God merely as a moral legislator, and for this reason urgently needed a better understanding of God's word. Luther therefore distinguished two ways in which God speaks to people: by commandments ('You shall ...') and by promises – or in Luther's terminology: God speaks to people in the way of the law and in the way of the Gospel.

Law and Gospel

Luther considered himself to be following St Paul in his distinction between the law and the Gospel. This distinction expresses a fundamental twofold experience with the word of God:

> *There are two things, which are presented to us in the word of God: either the wrath of God or the grace of God, sin or righteousness, death or life, hell or heaven.* (WA 39/1, 361, 4–6)

Luther did not want to separate the word of God into two parts or bring them into opposition. Nor did he wish to divide the biblical texts into two parts: the texts of the law and texts of the Gospel. For Luther, the distinction between law and Gospel represents different ways of seeing God's relationship to human beings. Luther sees God as speaking to people in two ways: on the one hand, demanding from them and commanding them, and on the other, making promises to them. These will now be looked at in turn.

THE DIVINE LAW

Luther distinguished at least two different uses of the divine law. First, God's word as law convicts people of their sin, and secondly, God's commandments are concerned with the proper ordering of human life, i.e. in framing rules which help to regulate and govern human society. The first function of the divine law Luther called its theological use, the second he called the political use of the law of God.

The first use of the divine law refers to the experience of God's holiness and justice which sets the standards for human life and opens the way for it to become holy and just. In the Old Testament the prophet Isaiah (6:5) describes his experience of the holiness of God, which Luther himself had experienced in 1507 when he first said the mass. Isaiah cried when he entered the Temple of God:

Woe is me! For I am lost ... for my eyes have seen the King, the Lord of hosts!

In the presence of God, everyone, even a prophet, experiences their own life as being unholy and worthless – a life that has to end and pass away.

God's holiness sets such a high standard for people that they feel unable to fulfil it. God's word as law therefore brings about in a person a realization that their present life does not meet the demands of the true, divine life. The law of God shows people that they stand convicted as sinners. In this sense the law of God does not lead directly to righteousness but exposes human sin, and with this uncovering of sin enables people to see themselves in their true state.

The commandments of God also serve a political purpose in that they help to order human life. God, as part of his creative activity, resists tendencies to chaos. There is, however, a difference between the ten commandments and, for example, the ordering of some procedures and rituals in the temple in Jerusalem. Thus Luther assumes that firstly there is the law of God, which was expressly revealed to Moses, and which is a general law not only for Jews but for all people – this divine law is written into the heart of human beings. Secondly there is in the biblical texts the Jewish law, which is valid only for the ordering of the life of the Jewish people.

The law of God, which God has written into the heart of human beings, is known by all people (compare Romans 2:14–15), and therefore it is older than the ten commandments of Moses. Luther considers that human beings know by nature that one has to worship God and love one's neighbour. This living law in the heart of human beings is identical with the law given by Moses and with the ethical commandments of the New Testament (especially Matthew 7:12: 'So whatever you wish that men would do to you, do so to them; for this is the law and the prophets').

Therefore there is one law which runs through all ages, is known to all men, is written in the hearts of people, and leaves no one from begin-ning to end with an excuse, although for the Jews ceremonies were added and the other nations had their own laws, which were not binding upon the whole world, but only this one, which the Holy Spirit dictates unceasingly in the hearts of all. (LECTURES ON GALATIANS (1519), LW 27, 355).

By this law human conscience is defined. The law, which is written in the heart of human beings by nature, utters itself in their conscience. In his or her conscience a person knows implic-itly the conditions that must be fulfilled for life to be worthy. Thus conscience is a divine voice in the midst of human life, but it is God as a legislator and a severe judge who speaks in conscience. In conscience a person is inexorably confronted by the demands of God and is accused and judged according to the measure of the divine law – and if this was all there was then the end would be desperation and death. Luther lived his own life based on con-science as the final and only judge, for example in his conduct before the Diet of Worms in 1521 (see p. 8). Luther has rendered the freedom of conscience a great service in the history of mankind. Like Thomas More (1477–1535), Luther made a stand on conscience, in the consciousness that before God he could not act otherwise (see in this series the book of Anne Murphy on *Thomas More*, pp. 56, 73–88). But it is God as the author of the divine law who speaks in conscience, and therefore conscience is part of the law to which human beings are subject. Conscience expresses the high dignity of the individual, but at the same time it expresses the fact that humans are not free. It is through failure to live up to one's conscience that one becomes aware of the need for God's grace.

But what are the demands of the law God has written in human hearts? Surely God not only makes demands on people by accus-ing and convicting them of sin, but has introduced rules – for example the ten commandments – to lay down the principles for an ordered life? For Luther, one of the functions of the political use of the divine law is to restrain crime in our sinful world, which is possessed by the devil, and by that to secure public peace. Commandments like 'You shall not kill', 'You shall not commit adultery' or 'You shall not steal' (Exodus 20:13–15) are examples of that. Other functions of the political use of the divine law are to arrange education and also, and most importantly, to make possible the preaching of the Gospel. Luther considered that God installs authorities and institutions, which have to transfer those fundamental laws into daily life and into political order. These institutions and authorities are the governments in the cities and countries, the civil law and especially the parents and teachers, because it is in the education of young people that foundations for the future are laid. With the help of these institutions and authorities, humans are able to fulfil the fundamental requirements of God for a peaceful and just order in society, because the alternative would be violence and chaos. It is of great importance for Luther that God has supplied a positive and beneficial order for human life in our fallen and sinful world. It is the will of God that people should live peacefully and in harmony with their neighbours. Reason, conscience and the law in human hearts are given by God, their creator, as the conditions necessary for an ordered, just and peaceful society.

On a critical note, it has to be said that there is a tendency for Luther to approve unquestioningly the existing political structures. He seems to consider that provided there is law and order and the word of God can be preached without restrictions, then the political situation should be accepted by Christians. Today we might consider that this is not an adequate specification of a good political system.

It is essential for Luther that people are confronted with both the demands of God in their lives and with the threat of despair. Confrontation with God's law makes it obvious to individuals that they are incapable of coming into a right relationship with God by their own efforts. Only when people come to realize the inadequacy of these efforts, will they then be ready to receive the Gospel. Only when an individual comes to despair and realizes that he or she cannot rely on their own strength does God then give them everything that they themselves could not produce by their own efforts; that is life in its fullness, as proclaimed in the Gospel.

THE GOSPEL

In the Gospel God addresses human beings as a gracious and kind God. The Gospel should not be seen as some sort of concession by God to people who cannot live up to the law, in the sense that God might say: 'My dear child, you do not manage to fulfil my law, but I forgive your failure and shall accept and love you as you are.' This would be a false understanding of Luther's position. When offering forgiveness, justice and love in the Gospel, God not only accepts the situation of people as they are, he also wants to change this for the good. The Gospel does not legitimate the present situation of life. God's aim in the Gospel and in the law are the same.

> *Here the second part of Scripture comes to our aid, namely, the promises of God which declare the glory of God, saying, 'If you wish to fulfil the law and not covet, as the law demands, come, believe in Christ in whom grace, righteousness, peace, liberty, and all things are promised you. If you believe, you shall have all things; if you do not believe, you shall lack all things.* (THE FREEDOM OF A CHRISTIAN, LW 31, 348–49)

The objectives of the divine law and the Gospel are for good things such as justice, peace and freedom, which are important for the whole of a person's life. But the Gospel not only formulates these aims, it already includes the realization of them, because they are realized in God. Once a person believes and trusts in God's promise then he or she will have everything God has promised, because in faith he or she takes part in the divine life. The Gospel therefore requires a response of faith, and it is faith alone that is needed to achieve the objectives. It is Luther's claim, that in believing the Gospel the believers *have* the 'spiritual' goods of peace, justice and freedom because they are made just, free, peaceful etc., by God.

Faith

Faith is the only way in which a person can respond to and honour God:

> So when the soul firmly trusts God's promises, it regards him as truthful and righteous. Nothing more excellent than this can be ascribed to God. The very highest worship of God is this, that we ascribe to him truthfulness, righteousness, and whatever else should be ascribed to one who is trusted. When this is done, the soul consents to God's will. Then it hallows God's name and allows itself to be treated according to God's good pleasure for, clinging to God's promises, it does not doubt that the One who is true, just, and wise will do, dispose, and provide all things well . . . On the other hand, what greater rebellion against God, what greater wickedness, what greater contempt of God is there than not believing his promise? For what is this but to make God a liar or to doubt that he is truthful? – that is, to ascribe truthfulness to oneself but lying and vanity to God?
> (THE FREEDOM OF A CHRISTIAN, LW 31, 350)

It is only through their faith in God that people can respond to and honour God. In their faith and their trust in God people let God be their god. For Luther this is the only way to fulfil the first of the ten commandments, which says: 'I am the Lord your God. You shall have no other gods before me' (Exodus 20:2–3). Therefore Luther wrote in the explanation of the first commandment in his *Large Catechism* in 1529:

If your faith and trust are right, then your God is the true God. On the other hand, if your trust is false and wrong, then you have not the true God. For these two belong together, faith and God. That to which your heart clings and entrusts itself is, I say, really your God. (WHAT DOES THIS MEAN? 57)

Faith is a matter of the heart of a person. Luther knows this subjective approach can be misleading, because people can have trust in something other than God and make that to be their god. True faith, therefore, involves the single-minded search for something really trustworthy, and this can only be found in God. In a lecture in 1535 on St Paul's letter to the Galatians, Luther set out the significance of true faith in the life of a believer. Interpreting Galatians 3:6 ('Thus Abraham believed God, and it was reckoned to him as righteousness') he says:

Faith is something omnipotent, and ... its power is inestimable and infinite; for it attributes glory to God, which is the highest thing that can be attributed to Him. To attribute glory to God is to believe in Him, to regard Him as truthful, wise, righteous, merciful, and almighty, in short, to acknowledge Him as the Author and Donor of every good. Reason does not do this, but faith does. It consummates the Deity; and, if I may put it this way, it is the creator of the Deity, not in the substance of God but in us. (LW 26, 227)

It is only through faith that the truth of God becomes vivid and real in people. One of the most rigorous modern critics of religion, the German philosopher Ludwig Feuerbach (1804–1872), saw in Luther's writing ('faith is the creator of the Deity') justification for his claim that God is a human projection. However, this was not Luther's position – he was a philosophic realist who believed that God created and sustains the universe. God does not exist because people believe in, speak to or talk about God. However, God only becomes a reality in human beings if they have faith. Attempts in theology and philosophy to think about God as the ultimate principle of all being, as the ultimate value, or as the first cause etc., do not satisfy Luther, as they do not incorporate a personal relationship of the believer to God. God cannot be thought about only as one more fact. Through faith, God has to become a living reality for people.

Faith comes about by each person being addressed by God's word in his or her heart. For Luther faith is a matter of the heart, that is, a matter for the individual, and he often exemplified that personal dimension of faith by pointing to a person's death. In a sermon in 1522 he said:

> *The summons of death comes to us all, and no one can die for another. Everyone must fight his own battle with death by himself, alone. We can shout into another's ear, but every one must himself be prepared for the time of death, for I will not be with you then, nor you with me. Therefore every one must himself know and be armed with the chief things which concern a Christian.* (LW 51, 70)

A believer cannot trust another or any authority, not even the Church and its representatives, when it comes to faith. He or she cannot say, 'If they believe it, it must be right.' Such a belief will not endure when faced by death. Only a personal faith will be creative, life-changing and liberating. But what are the characteristics of such a new life in faith, and what is in the very centre of Christian faith? Faith consists in placing Jesus Christ at the centre of one's life. To be a Christian is to belong to Christ.

6

Jesus Christ and Salvation

Luther was not satisfied with the mere theological formulation that Jesus was fully God and fully man although, of course, he accepted this. Faith goes beyond words, and it is the personal relationship to God and Jesus Christ which is of fundamental importance. Luther gives central place to the credal affirmation: 'I believe, that Jesus Christ ... is *my* Lord.' Luther did not totally reject the metaphysical definitions of Jesus Christ which were developed from concepts in Platonic and Aristotelian thought, and which have been part of the Christian confession of faith since the fifth century. However, a doctrine such as the two natures of Christ seems to define Jesus Christ without taking into account the benefits brought to each individual. Luther subordinates such definitions to the basic assertion which set Jesus Christ into relation with the person who believes, thus:

> *I believe, that Jesus Christ – true God, Son of the Father from eternity, and true man, born of the Virgin Mary – is my Lord.* (WHAT DOES THIS MEAN? 117)

For Luther, to seek Jesus Christ is to seek for God. In this he follows John's gospel, where Jesus is recorded as saying: 'He who has seen me has seen the Father' (John 14:9). Thus Luther says that looking at Jesus Christ we look:

> *... into the depth of the Father's heart, indeed, into the groundless and eternal kindness and love of God, which God offers to us continually, from all eternity.* (WA 20, 229, 13–15)

According to Luther the believer develops his or her knowledge of God by climbing steadily up from knowledge of Christ. The starting point of the ladder to God is the human being Jesus of Nazareth who is, for Luther, not simply a religious or moral ideal, but is truly human. Knowledge of God starts with knowledge of Jesus. After contemplating the suffering of Jesus Christ it is necessary to:

> *... pass beyond that and see his friendly heart and how his heart beats with such love for you that it impels him to bear with pain your conscience and your sin. Then your heart will be filled with love for him, and the confidence of your faith will be strengthened. Now continue and rise beyond Christ's heart to God's heart and you will see that Christ would not have shown this love for you if God in his eternal love had not wanted this, for Christ's love for you is due to his obedience to God. Thus you will find the divine and kind paternal heart, and, as Christ says, you will be drawn to the Father through him. Then you will understand the words of Christ, 'For God so loved the world that he gave his only Son, etc.' We know God aright when we grasp him not in his might or wisdom (for then he proves terrifying), but in his kindness and love. Then faith and confidence are able to exist, and then man is truly born anew in God.* (A MEDITATION ON CHRIST'S PASSION (1519), LW 42, 13)

Reflection on Jesus Christ provides insight into God's will. This basic principle of God's will is God's love for human beings and the world. Luther himself, however, challenges this concept and renders it problematic in some of his most impressive writings, for example, in *The Bondage of the Will* written in 1525, in answer to the critique of his theology in *The Freedom of the Will* by Erasmus.

One passage in Luther's *The Bondage of the Will* discusses the problem of predestination – why some people accept the grace of God and others reject it. If everything happens by God's will then why does God elect some people for salvation and exclude others? Luther, however, retreats behind mystery and says about 'that hidden and awful will of God whereby he ordains by his own counsel which and what sort of persons he wills to be recipients and partakers of his preached and offered mercy ...'

> ... *this will is not to be inquired into, but reverently adored, as by far the most awe-inspiring secret of the Divine Majesty, reserved for himself alone and forbidden to us.* (LW 33, 139)

Here we are confronted with one of the greatest problems in Luther's theology. His doctrine of God seems to become paradoxical if not almost contradictory, because he claims, as we have seen, that humans can know the divine will through Christ. It is hardly surprising that many theologians criticized Luther on this point. However, to do him justice we have to consider his position a bit further. The problem of predestination was raised by Erasmus: the problem is that if it is (as Luther claims) God's will which decides whether some accept and others despise God's offered grace, then a person is not free either to accept or reject this grace. Erasmus claimed, against Luther, that human beings are free either to accept or reject God and salvation, and that this decision is not determined by God. Human beings are free to accept or reject grace and to do everything necessary for a person's salvation through God. Luther's position gives rise to the question that Erasmus raises:

> *Does the good Lord deplore the death of his people, which he himself works in them?* (LW 33, 139)

To Luther, raising this question seems to be superficial and academic. As an alternative he proposes a certain hiddenness of God and from this follows:

> ... that we have to argue in one way about God or the will of God as preached, revealed, offered, and worshipped, and in another way about God as he is not preached, not revealed, not offered, not worshipped. To the extent, therefore, that God hides himself and wills to be unknown to us, it is no business of ours. For here the saying truly applies, 'Things above us are no business of ours'. (LW 33, 139)

Luther criticizes Erasmus for not distinguishing 'between God preached and God hidden, that is, between the Word of God and God himself' (LW 33, 140) as, Luther claims, Erasmus wants a consistent theological conception without paradoxes and intellectual problems. But for Luther much of life was full of paradoxes and problems which could not be solved. Thus Luther believed on the one hand that God's saving will was declared in God's word, but on the other hand he maintained that not all events are according to God's declared will. As an example, on the one hand God says 'I desire not the death of a sinner' (Ezekiel 18:23), but on the other hand it seems that God wills that certain people should reject his offer of grace and eternal life.

Does God thus cause people to be condemned? Luther's fellow reformer Jean Calvin in Geneva would have agreed that this is the case, because he thought that God not only elects who shall be saved, but also decides who shall be condemned. Luther rejected the latter position. However, he also rejected the view that it is up to human beings to decide whether or not to believe in God and whether or not to accept salvation. Luther believed that human reason cannot enable people to grasp and understand everything which happens in the course of their life. They cannot understand all the influences on them. In particular they cannot understand those hidden things which go beyond human understanding. For

Luther those 'things above' are hidden in God, who is above human understanding. That is God 'hidden in his majesty', who 'neither deplores nor takes away death, but works life, death, and all in all. For there he has not bound himself by his word, but has kept himself free over all things' (LW 33, 140).

Critics of Luther, such as the Swiss theologian Karl Barth (1886–1968), have pointed out that Luther's distinction between a revealed God and a hidden God brings him close to believing in two Gods, even though he did not intend this. Luther was a theologian who himself was in the midst of the conflicts and paradoxes of life – he recognized these conflicts but did not wish to dissolve them. The problem of the mysterious and hidden God remains a central problem for the whole of Luther's theology. But Luther's advice to believers shows the tendency he followed at least in spirituality:

> It is our business ... to pay attention to the word and leave that inscrutable will alone, for we must be guided by the word and not by that inscrutable will. (LW 33, 140)

This advice amounts to a call to have faith in Jesus Christ, who is God's self-revelation, and not to be concerned about an inability to comprehend divine mysteries or even be frightened by God who is hidden from human understanding. In saying this, Luther follows the view of his teacher and counsellor Johann von Staupitz, who had comforted him when his faith was placed on trial because of the possibility that God might not have elected him for heaven. In 1531 Luther reported about that: 'When I complained about such spiritual assaults to my good Staupitz, he replied, "I don't understand this; I know nothing about it" ' (LW 54, 133). Instead Staupitz advised him to cling to Jesus Christ alone. For Luther it is in Jesus Christ that we get to know God, and all efforts to know God through reason are doomed to failure. Luther criticized any philosophy that asserted its independence of God – but he used philosophy to clarify God's relations with human beings. Philosophy and human reason can never be self-sufficient because then reason is put first and the individual no longer listens to God. Philosophy's mistake is to start at the wrong point. Holy Scripture, by contrast:

> ... begins very cautiously and leads us to Christ like to a man and after that to a Lord over all creatures, after that to a God. Thus I come in easily and learn to know God. But philosophy and those people who are full of the wisdom of this world wanted to start from above; but then they have become fools. One has to start from below and then come up. (WA 10, 297, 5–10)

The points we have discussed so far in respect to Luther's understanding of Jesus Christ – our complete knowledge of God in Jesus Christ and the relation of Jesus Christ to the individual – are important for Luther to show that a living relationship with God is possible. Luther did not want to pin God down to orders and structures which human reason can conceive, but to acknowledge God's freedom.

In Jesus Christ God does not meet humanity in general, but concrete individuals. But what happens when Jesus Christ meets a person? What changes occur when a person encounters Christ? To talk about this is to talk of the salvation of a person through Jesus Christ.

To describe the uniting of Jesus Christ and an individual Luther made use of an image from St Paul's letter to the Ephesians (Ephesians 5:31–32). Luther writes in 1520 in *The Freedom of a Christian*, that faith:

> ... unites the soul with Christ as a bride is united with her bridegroom. By this mystery ... Christ and the soul become one flesh. And if they are one flesh and there is between them a true marriage ... it follows that everything they have they hold in common, the good as well as

the evil. Accordingly the soul can boast of and glory in whatever Christ has as though it were its own, and whatever the soul has Christ claims as his own ... Christ is full of grace, life, and salvation. The soul is full of sin, death, and damnation. Now let faith come between them and sin, death, and damnation will be Christ's, while grace, life, and salvation will be the soul's ... Here we have a most pleasing vision not only of communion but of a blessed struggle and victory and salvation and redemption. Christ is God and man in one person. He has neither sinned nor died, and is not condemned, and he cannot sin, die, or be condemned ... By the wedding ring of faith he shares in the sins, death, and pains of hell which are his bride's. As a matter of fact, he makes them his own and acts as if they were his own and as if he himself had sinned; he suffered, died, and descended into hell that he might overcome them all ... His righteousness is greater than the sins of all men, his life stronger than death, his salvation more invincible than hell. Thus the believing soul by means of the pledge of its faith is free in Christ, its bridegroom, free from all sins, secure against death and hell, and is endowed with the eternal righteousness, life, and salvation of Christ its bridegroom ... Here this rich and divine bridegroom, Christ, marries this poor, wicked harlot, redeems her from all her evil, and adorns her with all his goodness. Her sins cannot now destroy her, since they are laid upon Christ and swallowed up by him. And she has that righteousness in Christ, her husband, of which she may boast as of her own and which she can confidently display alongside her sins in the face of death and hell and say, 'If I have sinned, yet my Christ, in whom I believe, has not sinned, and all his is mine and all mine is his.' (LW 31, 351–352)

In this scene Luther pictures salvation. He describes a person becoming free from the past and, in being united with Jesus Christ, becoming a new and free person. The whole marriage of Jesus Christ and the human soul is a glorious and saving event, because Jesus Christ has never sinned nor will ever sin. The evil and sin of a human being cannot change Jesus Christ, but instead sin is engulfed by Christ's righteousness, which overpowers the sins of all. For believers it is essential that they put their whole trust in the promise that Jesus Christ totally overcomes sin, and gives humans a share in his glory, righteousness and freedom. This saving and renewing of humans can only take place if they have become united with God. In this encounter a person participates in the divine glory, righteousness and freedom.

7

The Priesthood of All Believers
and the Christian Church

The most important consequence of Luther's understanding of people's salvation through Christ was the doctrine of the priesthood of all believers. Luther abolished the distinction between priests and laity, and opened to all people the special relationship which previously existed only between the priest and God. According to Luther, every person may exercise the priestly office by relating directly to God.

Traditional religious opinion holds that a priest is a person who appears before God on behalf of others so that they may gain forgiveness and further divine blessings. In Christianity the priestly office was originally restricted to Jesus Christ, who by his death on the cross was the sacrifice which, once and for all, reconciled God with all people, and who, as the son of God, now appears before him and intercedes for mankind. The traditional priestly office was gradually introduced into the Christian Church as well, but restricted to the priests as an especially selected part of the Christian community. The priests were understood as representing Christ's mediating office here on earth. Luther rejected this idea and saw all believers as priests, because in faith they take part not only in the dignity of Christ but in his tasks and offices as well.

According to Luther, Jesus Christ has the offices of both priest and king. As king, Jesus rules all earthly affairs, and as priest he mediates between human beings and God. In both offices Jesus cares completely for people: for their earthly, bodily and spiritual well-being. But Jesus Christ is not a ruler and mediator remote from those for whom he is caring. He is the God who has come to all people and has devoted himself to them, and Jesus therefore shares with his believers all his goods and all his tasks, including his kingly and his priestly office.

In their faith believers become co-operators with the work and task of Jesus Christ: they become priests and kings. As priests they have the authority to forgive sins in the name of God, to spread the message of the grace of God and to invite people to the Lord's Supper. It is the duty of every Christian to perform priestly tasks and to mediate between human beings and God. That is the purpose of prayer and intercession for others. This new understanding of priesthood is an emancipation of people, because now the priestly office is no longer restricted to a special group of church members, but is open to all. Each person who appears before God in prayer and who intercedes for others is a priest.

To be a priest is to have spiritual power. To appear as a priest before God, asking God for help and interceding for others is not like an appeal to the benevolence of an emperor. According to Luther it is the other way round: in praying to God, in asking and interceding for others, one has power over God.

Who can comprehend the lofty dignity of the Christian? By virtue of his royal power he rules over all things, death, life, and sin, and through his priestly glory has power over God because God does the things which he asks and desires, as it is written, 'He will fulfil the desire of those who fear him; he also will hear their cry and save them'. (THE FREEDOM OF A CHRISTIAN, LW 31, 357)

This is a challenging position, because it can be held that for human beings to have 'power over God' is impossible. To avoid the problematic word 'over' some prefer to translate the Latin text as 'omnipotent with God'. For Luther this challenging position follows on from taking seriously God's own words, as Jesus promised that God would do all the things which we ask for and desire. To have 'power over God' or be 'omnipotent with God' therefore relates to the power of the Christian in prayer.

Luther's position is not that in prayer God is at the believer's disposal. It is characteristic of petitionary prayer that God's freedom is respected when believers ask for anything. When we ask someone for something, we show trust in them, that they will do and grant what we have asked. Similarly it is through trust and confidence in God that Luther talks of humans having power over God or being omnipotent with God in prayer. If we turn to God in total trust and faith then God will not deny our requests and prayers. In Luther's time this was a controversial idea. For Luther this omnipotence of believers in prayer was not dependent on the social, moral or religious status of people, but on the principle that everyone, including scoundrels, could have this power by turning to God in total trust and faith. With this interpretation of the priesthood of all believers, the traditional role of the priest is dramatically reduced, and God is directly accessible through the prayers of each person. The love of God is focused on each single individual, and no institution and no person can act for someone else in this relationship. Never before had the individual been taken so seriously and given such high dignity, and this is a legacy which Luther left to the Western world. This heritage has to be defended again and again against many political and religious developments, in which the importance and value of community is placed above that of individuals. This applies within the Christian Church as well, if there is a tendency to give priority to the community or the church as a group over the individual. The best that a church can do, according to Luther, is to help individuals develop their own relationships with God.

Why, then, did Luther consider that an institutional church and a professional ministry were still important? For Luther, their main purpose was to be an instrument for bringing about successful relationships between individuals and God. However, there are other aspects of his doctrine of the church. He spent much time developing a new, Protestant understanding of the Christian Church, and he had a great deal to do with the new organization of the life of the church. Luther had significant new understandings of the ministry of the church, the need to reform the liturgy of Christian worship, his new understanding of the eucharist, his writing of the two *Catechisms* for the education of believers in Christian doctrine, as well as his ideas about the unity of the Christian Church. In this book, however, there is no space to consider these important aspects of his teaching. But it is significant briefly to review Luther's appraisal of the relationship between the different Christian churches, as this is important today in the field of ecumenical dialogue.

In his doctrine of the church Luther distinguished between the one universal, invisible Church of Jesus Christ and the many visible churches, namely the different organizations and confessions like the Protestant, Roman Catholic and Orthodox churches. For Luther those organizations, which might operate worldwide or only locally or regionally, are mainly justified in their function as a means for nurturing individual Christian faith and life and for further spreading the Gospel. Beyond their differences there is a unity of the churches which is founded in God, and is expressed in worship, in the preaching of the word of God and in the main sacraments. In Christian worship and in the giving of the sacraments (sacraments here being baptism and the Lord's Supper) the invisible community of all believers is present. Luther was convinced that the Christian Church is everywhere on earth where the Gospel of Jesus Christ is preached and the sacraments are administered. People are not united as the Christian Church because of their membership of an institutional church but because of their common faith and common trust in God. It is this community which finds its expression in every act of Christian worship, being a reality where people celebrate in worship, where the Gospel of Jesus Christ is preached and where the sacraments are received.

If the true community of all Christians, which is manifest in public Christian worship, is questioned, then the unity of the Christian churches really is in danger. This happens, for example, by one church excluding from the eucharist Christians who are members of other churches. Bread and wine as the body and blood of Jesus Christ have to be administered to everyone who comes forward for them. By excluding certain believers from the eucharist, a church's own existence should be questioned because it is failing to fulfil the message of the gospels. Such a church fails to be the Church of Jesus Christ, because in behaving in such a manner, a human-made law is made to dominate the Gospel of the saving grace of God.

8

The Christian Life

Luther's understanding of the priesthood of all believers gives rise to his very positive understanding of the Christian as one who participates in the dignity of Jesus Christ. The first characteristic of such a Christian life is **freedom**, the second is **love**. In *The Freedom of a Christian* Luther summed this up in a famous phrase:

> A Christian is a perfectly free lord of all, subject to none.
> A Christian is a perfectly dutiful servant of all, subject to all.
> (LW 31, 344)

Freedom

Freedom is the central feature of a Christian. Through faith in God people can gain freedom. Without such faith and trust human beings, in Luther's understanding, are not free, because they are captive within themselves. Through God coming into a loving relationship with each individual they gain freedom from earthly constraints. Luther himself gave a good example of his understanding of Christian freedom when he refused to withdraw his theological convictions before the German Diet in the city of Worms in 1521. Obligated only to the word of God, Luther was free to withstand all authorities and their threats. But this individual independence is not the only consequence of a Christian's freedom. A Christian also becomes free from his or her own desires and the covetous drive to possess as many earthly goods as possible.

However Christian freedom relates to the things of this world – the Christian is not free in relation to God. Christians are bound to God and their earthly freedom comes precisely from their bondage to God. As we have seen, Luther rejected the position of Erasmus that it is up to each individual's free will to accept or to reject God's offered grace. Luther, following Augustine, instead claims that human beings owe their salvation entirely to God. Human beings are totally corrupted, because they are totally bound to their own individual interests and abilities, and therefore do not think that they need God and God's salvation in their lives. It follows from this that people make themselves captive and lose their freedom – they have to be liberated from their self-imposed chains, and this can only be done by God.

If people are bound to the word of God and trust in it, they then become free in respect to everything and everybody on earth. However, Christian freedom is not a once-and-for-all affair – Luther considered it to be under continuous threat. This freedom is challenged every day because human nature still has the tendency to put individual interests, desires and covetousness first in life, and therefore there is an in-built tendency to un-freedom, to becoming bound once more by the chains of sin.

In defining a Christian as 'a perfectly free lord of all' and 'a perfectly dutiful servant of all' Luther follows St Paul, who in his first letter to the Corinthians claims: 'For though I am free from all men, I have made myself a slave to all' (1 Corinthians 9:19). For Luther, as for Paul, it was no contradiction to understand Christians as being free and independent, yet at the same time as binding themselves to others and serving them. This follows because, Luther considered, freedom means in particular to be free from themselves: free people are not bound to themselves but may step back from themselves. People who believe in God, and who therefore share in the fullness of the divine life, are free because they have to do nothing for themselves. Everything essential for life has already been done for them by God. Because they are free. Christians are able to begin something new, for example to initiate new relationships or restore old ones by forgiveness and reconciliation. Christians as free people share in the divine creativity. Only a free person is able to give true love, that is free love: a love which does not insist on its own way, but seeks the best interests of others. Freedom and love are like a couple or the two sides of the same coin. We now turn to that other side of the coin – to Luther's understanding of love and the Christian's responsibility for the common life.

Love and Responsibility

The basis of Luther's ethics is his doctrine of the two realms. According to one version of this doctrine (which is not identical with Luther's view), God rules over a heavenly and an earthly realm according to principles, rules and laws which are specific for each of those two realms. In the heavenly realm the principle of the Gospel is valid: this realm is ruled by divine grace. In the earthly realm, with our concrete human conditions of life, God rules by law and through human reason. Therefore as regards the best ordering of all affairs in society and between individuals Christians cannot contribute their insights about the grace of God.

This version of Luther's 'two realms' doctrine is too simple an account of his thought. His ethics are not based on a strict separation of a heavenly and an earthly realm. When in 1520 Luther wrote *To the Christian Nobility of the German Nation Concerning the Reform of the Christian Estate* (LW 44, 115–217) this was intended to convince the German princes of the need for a reformation of the Church. In it, he appealed to Christians in government to take responsibility for the progress of the Reformation and for a good common order. With regard to the actions of individual Christians it is undoubtedly true that these should be motivated and called forth by their faith. In *The Freedom of a Christian* we read:

> *I will therefore give myself as a Christ to my neighbour, just as Christ offered himself to me. I will do nothing in this life except what I see is necessary, profitable, and salutary for my neighbour, since through faith I have an abundance of all good things in Christ. Behold, from faith flows forth love and joy in the Lord, and from love a joyful, willing, and free mind that serves one's neighbour willingly and takes no account of gratitude or ingratitude, of praise or blame, of gain or loss ... Hence, as our heavenly Father has in Christ freely come to our aid, we also ought freely to help our neighbour through our body and its works, and each one should become as it were a Christ to the other that we may be Christs to one another and Christ may be the same in all, that is, that we may be truly Christians.* (LW 31, 367–68)

If good works, deeds and actions for our fellow humans are not done freely, willingly and spontaneously, then love is missing. It is the essence of love to concentrate wholly on the other person, on the beloved and not on oneself. An act of love is characterized by forgetting oneself and having only the other person in mind. Luther wants to emphasize this essence of love, and the true essence of faith as well, when he distinguishes between faith in God and good human works and actions. Luther claims that if we do something good, it should be done for others. The good we do should not be intended to bring praise for ourselves or to give our own life some kind of meaning. If we do something good to other people we should look on ourselves as people of no account. It is a misuse of love when help to others is intended to serve self-interest – for example, by bringing praise to ourselves or salving our own consciences. A good action must be wholly selfless.

Luther's doctrine of justification by faith alone, without good works, can be seen to challenge each individual to ask whether we genuinely live only for the good of others by showing non-preferential love or whether our real motive for our supposedly good actions is pride in our own self-righteousness. Luther wishes each person to probe the motives for his or her own actions – he praises love that does not seek the good of the one who loves but which genuinely seeks the good of the other person alone, even though this may be costly. Luther's emphasis on genuine, true and unconditional love presents a real challenge for every person, because most people, he feels, fail to act in the unselfish manner which genuine love demands.

The challenge to conform truly to such a demand to love remains throughout the life of each individual, and all Christians constantly fail to live up to it. It is for this reason that the grace of God is needed throughout the whole of an individual's life. Again and again each person has to put their trust in God, who is devoted unconditionally to them. Luther considers that Christians are expected to transfer their experience of receiving the saving love of God into their daily lives. For him, faith is not simply a private matter – it has to be lived out in the day-to-day activities of life.

Luther dealt with many practical questions. He wrote on the problems of private and public life, for example on public education, on economic problems, on legal questions and on general political problems. Two examples of Luther's ethics, which well illustrate the doctrine of two realms, are worthy of examination here: firstly Luther's understanding of vocation, and secondly his approach to sexuality and marriage.

Vocation

Luther rejected the idea that priests and monks have a 'higher' or more holy occupation than those who undertake 'worldly' jobs. In his writing *On Monastic Vows* (1521) he rejects the high spiritual status accorded to monks as being the only group called. He quotes 1 Corinthians 7:20: 'Every one should remain in the state to which he was called', and argues that normal working people are undertaking tasks which are approved by

God and good in themselves. For Luther, a 'calling' does not mean to be called out of the world but to be called into service in the world where one is needed. All work, however, should be undertaken as a work of love and to honour and serve God, recognizing the contribution one is making to other people. The office of the priest is, essentially, no different from that of the road sweeper, for both are undertaking worthwhile and important tasks in the service of God and society at large. Whether or not a person does a job well can be judged by reason and by worldly standards of measurement. What it means to work successfully and well will depend on the chosen career or calling, but success in this task is to be measured by ordinary, human means and not by appeal to theological or spiritual principles. Having said this, there is a spiritual dimension to all work since it is undertaken in the service of God and out of love for one's neighbour. As Luther said in a sermon:

> If everyone serves his neighbour, then the world would be full of worship. (WA 36, 340, 12–13)

A high standard of education is important to equip young people for lives of service. In Luther's time, there was a strict class system, and Luther did not really challenge this. However, because of his stress on individual responsibility he considered that education for all was vital, and he argued that, through education, all walks of life might be open to young people. There are here, therefore, at least the seeds of a more egalitarian approach to society, although Luther did not develop them further. In 'A Sermon on Keeping Children in School' (1530) Luther said that the task of education was 'to take beggars and make them into lords'. He went on to say:

> It is not God's will that only those who are born kings, princes, lords, and nobles should exercise rule and lordship. He wills to have his

> *beggars among them also, lest they think it is nobility of birth rather*
> *than God alone who makes lords and rulers.* (LW 46, 250)

Luther believed that all children should be educated, and called for grants to be given by governments and churches to make this possible. The objective was to produce future generations who would live lives of service to God and their neighbour.

Sexuality and Marriage

Luther rejected the idea that priests should have to remain celibate. His early remarks on sex and marriage were made against the background of his knowledge of the problems which many monks and priests had with celibate life. Luther considered sexuality to be part of human nature and to have been created by God, and therefore rejected the heritage of the Middle Ages, which had seen all sexual activity as tainted and as an aspect of the base part of human beings, to be undertaken solely as a duty for the purpose of procreation (cf. *The Puzzle of Sex*, Peter Vardy, Harper-Collins, 1997). For Luther the love of a man and a woman can be contrasted with false love and with natural love – married love can be the greatest and purest of all loves, and there was no reason why a priest should not be married, nor would marriage detract from the exercise of the priestly office. In 'A Sermon on the Estate of Marriage' (1519) Luther writes:

> *False love is that which seeks its own, as a man loves money, posses-*
> *sions, honour, and women taken outside marriage and against God's*
> *command. Natural love is that between father and child, brother and*
> *sister, friend and relative, and similar relationships. But over and*
> *above all these is married love, that is, a bride's love, which glows like*
> *a fire and desires nothing but the husband. She says, 'It is you I want,*
> *not what is yours: I want neither your silver nor your gold; I want*
> *neither. I want only you. I want you in your entirety, or not at all.' All*

other kinds of love seek something other than the loved one: this kind wants only to have the beloved's own self completely. If Adam had not fallen, the love of bride and groom would have been the loveliest thing.
(LW 44, 9)

However, Adam did fall and with him all human beings. This means that even 'married love' is no longer flawless:

... now this love is not pure either, for admittedly a married partner desires to have the other, yet each seeks to satisfy his desire with the other, and it is this desire which corrupts this kind of love. Therefore, the married state is now no longer pure and free from sin. (LW 44, 9)

Luther followed Augustine and considered that because of the Fall, physical desire had become such a strong force that it challenged the will of human beings. It was such a strong force that it was impossible for human beings to remain virginal and chaste without the special grace of God. In an essay on 'The Estate of Marriage' (1522), Luther, following Matthew 19:12, defined three categories of people, who possibly could remain without a spouse:

There are eunuchs, who have been so from birth, and there are eunuchs who have been made eunuchs by men, and there are eunuchs who have made themselves eunuchs for the sake of the kingdom of heaven. (LW 45, 18)

In Luther's time, the third category was particularly significant, as many young men and women went into a monastery or were sent there by their families even though they had normal sexual desires. Luther considered that such persons who are naturally inclined towards marriage by nature but who nevertheless voluntarily remain celibate, 'are rare, not one in a thousand, for they are a special miracle of God'. He goes on to say:

> *No one should venture on such a life unless he be especially called by*
> *God ... or unless he finds God's grace to be so powerful within him that*
> *the divine injunction, 'Be fruitful and multiply', has no place in him.*
> (LW 45, 21)

Luther's comments had dramatic consequences. Many monks and nuns felt free to accept that they had not been called to celibacy but instead to normal married life – they had been called, in other words, to follow the divine injunction to 'Be fruitful and multiply'. Hundreds left their monasteries. Luther writes:

> *No vow of any youth or maiden is valid before God, except that of a*
> *person in one of the three categories which God alone has himself*
> *excepted. Therefore, priests, monks, and nuns are duty-bound to*
> *forsake their vows whenever they find that God's ordinance to produce*
> *seed and to multiply is powerful and strong within them. They have no*
> *power by any authority, law, command, or vow to hinder this which*
> *God has created within them. If they do hinder it, however, you may*
> *be sure that they will not remain pure but inevitably besmirch them-*
> *selves with secret sins or fornication. For they are simply incapable of*
> *resisting the word and ordinance of God within them.* (LW 45, 19)

If people are not especially called to celibacy, it is normal for them to follow their sexual inclination and interest. Luther saw that many priests and monks could not resist their natural instincts, and therefore broke their vows in secret and thus fell deeper into sin. It was better for them, he considered, to marry, because marriage then 'may be likened to a hospital for incurables which prevents inmates from falling into graver sin' (A SERMON ON THE ESTATE OF MARRIAGE, LW 44, 9).

In that sense marriage is partly a kind of emergency measure to prevent people from perverting their sexuality. For Luther, only within marriage can sex not lead people away from God or even destroy a person and his or her relations with others. However, this is not the whole story as marriage was also ordained and blessed by God before the Fall. God intended marriage so that the world could be populated and also so that men and women should enjoy their love of each other.

To Luther, marriage is not a sacrament: it is not a means by which people are saved and take part in divine life. Marriage, however, is an institution which is blessed by God. The effect of this teaching was that the new Protestant churches that followed Luther abandoned to the state their jurisdiction over the legal side of the marriage. A couple first had to get married in a civil cere-mony and then would receive the blessing in church. Marriage is a worldly affair, and as part of the natural order of the world has to follow the jurisdiction of the state.

Marriage is a good example of the doctrine of the two realms. It is part of the natural order of the world and therefore has to be organized according to the principles of nature and of reason. People do not need to get married in order to find salvation – marriage is merely one answer to the question of how human life should be lived and does not contribute to an understanding of a human individual's relationship to God. However, the kingdom of this world, of nature, of which marriage forms part, is never-theless still ruled by God. Although all matters within the natural realm are organized by human beings using their reason, this realm is still created and blessed by God. Marriage is part of the order of nature and is ordained by God for the good of human beings. It may not be a part of the way to God, but it is still an important institution and a means of helping people find the form of life most adequate to the needs and desires of their nature.

After being married himself in 1525 Luther's statements about marriage and family life changed in tone. Before his own marriage he emphasized the natural instincts of people in sexuality and marriage, but afterwards he laid more stress on the different aspects of a marriage and the role of his wife, Katherine. Luther did not marry Katherine because he had fallen in love. In a letter of June 1525 he gives some reasons for his marriage. He writes:

The rumour is true that I was suddenly married to Katherine; [I did this] to silence the evil mouths which are so used to complaining about me. For I still hope to live for a little while. In addition, I also did not want to reject this unique [opportunity to obey] my father's wish for progeny, which he so often expressed. At the same time, I also wanted to confirm what I have taught by practising it ... God has willed and brought about this step. For I feel neither passionate love nor burning for my spouse, but I cherish her. (LW 49, 117)

For Luther, merely to be in love was an inadequate basis for marriage. In table talk in the winter of 1542–1543 Luther said:

We hate the things that are present and we love those that are absent ... This is the weakness of our nature ... It's easy enough to get a wife, but to love her with constancy is difficult ... Accordingly if a man intends to take a wife, let him be serious about it and pray to God, 'Dear Lord God ... bestow upon me a good, pious girl with whom I may spend all my life, whom I hold dear, and who loves me.' There is more to it than a union of the flesh. There must be harmony with respect to patterns of life and ways of thinking. (LW 54, 444)

Luther himself was susceptible to the beauty of other women. Even a few days before his death, while he was away from home staying at Eisleben, he wrote to his wife, probably partly to needle her:

Thank God now I am well, except for the fact that beautiful women tempt me so much that I neither care nor worry about becoming unchaste. (LW 50, 291)

When such temptations occurred Luther considered it important to remember that it was God who had given the existing husband or wife. However, Luther also recognized that if a couple were to remain faithful it was necessary for their sexual needs to be satisfied – marriage had to fulfil two functions: the one is to have and to educate children, and the second is that the two people living together should share everything. Sexual intercourse is not only intended for procreation but is a natural part and expression of the love of a couple. In that he criticizes the view of St Paul, when he writes in his essay on 'The Estate of Marriage' (1522):

> *Although Christian married folk should not permit themselves to be governed by their bodies in the passion of lust, as Paul writes to the Thessalonians (1 Thessalonians 4:5), nevertheless each one must examine himself so that by his abstention he does not expose himself to the danger of fornication and other sins.* (LW 45, 36)

In saying this, Luther was accepting and emphasizing the idea of sex as a duty, with both parties under a moral obligation to provide physical access to the other. Refusal of sexual intercourse could, it was traditionally held, lead to sin, and Luther accepted this view.

Luther had a traditional understanding of married life. The man was head of the family and represented it to the outside world. However, his concept of family life is open to accommodate different social circumstances. Katherine not only had responsibility for running the house but for the finances of the family as well, whilst her husband concentrated on his tasks at university and in the wider public arena. Both partners were responsible for the education of children, and, indeed, Luther's own children often played in his study whilst he was working.

9

The Concept of Theology

At the end of this survey of central ideas in Martin Luther's thought, it is important to consider his understanding of the role of theology. Theology, Luther considered, is characterized especially by its content and its subject. For him:

> *The proper subject of theology is man guilty of sin and condemned, and God the Justifier and Saviour of man the sinner. Whatever is asked or discussed in theology outside this subject, is error and poison.*
> (LW 12, 311)

For Luther theology is always concerned with knowledge of God and of human beings in the specific sense which is given in the biblical texts. The subject of theology is not simply God, but the relation between guilty and condemned human beings and the God who justifies and saves. Anything else may have limited interest but it is not part of theology. As an example, consideration of God alone without taking notice of God's relation to people; or a consideration of human beings without their relationship to God would not be theology in Luther's eyes. The mutual relationship between the divine and the human is of paramount importance. Luther considers Jesus Christ to be a proper subject for theological study, because in Jesus Christ sinful and condemned human beings and the justifying and saving God come together. It is through knowledge of Jesus Christ, especially of the *crucified* Jesus Christ, that we get to know that specific quality of the relation of human beings and God. According to Luther, the true understanding of Jesus Christ is found not in the incarnation, but in the crucifixion. On the cross the true relation of God and human beings becomes visible, and it is there that we can arrive at true knowledge of God and of ourselves.

In 1518 in the Heidelberg disputation and subsequently, especially in his work on the interpretation of the psalms in 1519–1521, Luther used the concept of a *theologia crucis* (a theology of the cross), which he had derived from monastic spirituality:

> *That person does not deserve to be called a theologian who looks upon the invisible things of God as though they were clearly perceptible in those things which have actually happened. He deserves to be called a theologian, however, who comprehends the visible and manifest things of God seen through suffering and the cross ... A theology of the cross calls the thing what it actually is.* (THE HEIDELBERG DISPUTATION, LW 31, 40)

The possibility is set out by St Paul in Romans 1:20, that:

> *... ever since the creation of the world God's invisible nature, namely, his eternal power and deity, has been clearly perceived in the things that have been made.*

Luther relates this to paradise and the time before Adam's fall. For people here on earth after Adam's fall, all that they can know is that God exists – they can have, using their own natural abilities, no knowledge of the essence of God. They cannot, therefore, know whether God is kind or frightening, loving or terrifying. For Luther this is true for all theological attempts to deduce knowledge of God from his creation by using reason alone. This was the approach taken by Philosophical Theology which sought to arrive not only at God's existence but also at basic knowledge about God's attributes using reason alone. Luther terms all such attempts a theology of glory, and claims that people are trying to use reason and their own abilities to grasp the majesty of God. They will necessarily fail in this task – they may see the products of the glory of God but not God himself.

The alternative approach to theology Luther sees as a theology of the cross, which concentrates on the death of the Son of God. Luther wants to understand the crucifixion of the Son of God and what this event reveals about God. In this event God's glory and majesty is hidden under what appears to be exactly the opposite: the living and creative God is hidden in the death of Jesus Christ.

Luther's theology takes seriously both the positive and the negative side of the human experience of life. Luther knew from his own experience – for example, the early death of two of his children – that life is not always successful and happy, and that the activity of a good, merciful, kind, just and loving God is by no means obvious. If one attempts to know God from God's works or by way of rational argument from earthly phenomena, then it is far from obvious that one will arrive at the Christian understanding of God. Any being recognized by such methods could as well be the devil as God. Luther is far too down-to-earth to ignore the negative sides of life in formulating his theology. He is clear that the world contains beauty and glory but also ugliness, cruelty and suffering. In the death of Jesus Christ, the creative and loving God has taken part in the darker side of human experience of a life ending in pain, despair and death. God, therefore, is not revealed through God's works in God's mighty power but rather is revealed in weakness.

Just as God's presence is hidden on the cross, so God is hidden in the human experience of suffering and evil. Luther's theology accepts the bitter side of life and does not attempt to explain it away. However, his refusal to attempt to overcome the tension between the frequent sadness, loneliness, pain and hurt which characterize so much of the human experience of life, and Christian talk of a loving and merciful God, leads to further theological problems. Luther can, in fact, be characterized as working with two concepts of God – the God of revelation and the idea of a hidden and undisclosed God. Luther recognizes this tension but refuses to compromise either of the two views in order to overcome it. Throughout his life Luther was uncompromisingly honest in his thinking, and he would neither sacrifice any part of the truth of Holy Scripture nor reduce his recognition of the bleakness of the concrete experience of human life. Rather he accepted difficulties and paradoxes. He would have accepted much of the writings of Søren Kierkegaard, a Danish Lutheran and probably the greatest philosopher of the nineteenth century, who wrote on paradoxes:

> However one should not think slightingly of the paradoxical; for the paradox is the source of the thinker's passion, and the thinker without a paradox is like a lover without feeling; a paltry mediocrity ... The supreme passion of all thought is the attempt to discover something that thought cannot think ... (PHILOSOPHIC FRAGMENTS, TRANSLATED BY DAVID SWENSON, PRINCETON UNIVERSITY PRESS, 46)

For Kierkegaard, Jesus Christ as true God and true Man was 'the Absolute Paradox', and Luther's thought was rooted in paradoxes. However, he did not see the revealed God and the hidden God as contradicting each other. Rather they were held in tension: they might appear to be contradictory but in fact were not. Luther thought in terms of the unity of God, which is the reason why the death of the Son of God is central to his theology.

In Luther's understanding, God, the creator and preserver of life, is hidden in the suffering and dying Jesus. This means for him that God is not absent but present in the cruelty of the crucifixion, which opposes everything for which God stands. The same is true for all the suffering and evil people experience: human beings are not left to their own devices, they are not alone in their suffering – God is present in these and God is also hidden. For Luther it would have been terrifying to assume that there are parts of life where God is not present, as this would have meant the abandonment of those parts of human existence to the devil. Luther preferred to accept and live with the very real and unresolved problem of exactly *how* God is present in death and suffering, rather than to believe that God was absent from them and had abandoned these areas of life. In Luther's view, evil will not have the final word. As Alister E. McGrath (*Luther's Theology of the Cross*) has pointed out, Luther's theology of the hidden presence and of the hidden work of God in the world is a theology of hope for all those who despair over suffering.

It is due to Luther taking seriously the negative experience of life, in which God is not seen as the creator and preserver of life, that he rejects the idea of any theology based on the glory of God. Instead he focuses on a theology of the cross. A positive theology of glory which starts by praising God the creator and his creative majesty would also result in praising human beings, as well as their rational and moral characteristics. This implies a generally positive understanding of human beings which Luther rejected. Luther's refusal to see human beings in a positive light is due to his view that this represents a subtle version of the idea that human beings can be justified by their works rather than by their faith and trust in God. Luther's alternative aims not only to arrive at a true understanding of God but also of human beings. Above all he wishes to guard against the human propensity to overestimate themselves and their own abilities. The way to God does not, for Luther, represent a religious ascent of the individual through the practice of good works and gradually growing intellectual awareness of God. Instead it is characterized by a receptiveness to God and God's word. A person can become open to God not through personal religious efforts and practices but in coming to see their own worthlessness and helplessness and the extent of their reliance on God's goodness and love. Concentration on the Cross of Christ was not a theological invention of Luther's own, it has been present throughout Christian history. Luther's theology is distinctive, however, in that, starting from the Cross, he does not lead people away from worldly affairs but takes them even deeper into all the uncertainty and contingency of the reality of human life.

Luther did not consider theology to be a theoretical but a practical discipline, because its knowledge is not about God and God's activities unrelated to human life. He rather considers God in relationship to human beings. Practical knowledge of theology has to be combined with a kind of passivity, in which people can be still and yet attentive to hear and receive God and his word – and to do nothing more. Passivity is not the same as showing no interest, but means only to dispense with our own activities for the sake of an ever higher concentration and attention to God. Doing theology means investing one's own life in the enterprise – one cannot do theology as a detached observer. Because of this, a personal risk is always involved: the risk of involving one's own personal life in the search for truth and understanding about human beings in relation to God. If one is unwilling to embark on this quest, one will not be able to do theology as Luther envisaged it. Theology, therefore, is quite the opposite from a boring, irrelevant subject concerned with dusty texts and ancient ideas and doctrines – it is rather to do with understanding God and human beings in their relation to each other.

Theology will always continue and develop as long as the story of God's relationship with human beings continues. It is an ongoing exploration process. Theology arises out of a lived faith which is tested time and again. In Luther's understanding it is essential that an individual's faith should be challenged if he or she is to be a theologian. In the introduction to *The Freedom of a Christian* Luther writes about Christian faith:

> *It is impossible to write well about it or to understand what has been written about it unless one has at one time or another experienced the courage which faith gives a man when trials oppress him.* (LW 31, 343)

For Luther no one can be a theologian who is not related existentially to God, and whose faith has not been tested by the fact that his or her faith does not appear to correspond to his or her experiences in the world. When a person, in a concrete situation, finds themselves unable to trust in the Gospel and promises of God, Luther considers this to be a trial of their faith and their relation to God. The same happens when God's love and grace remain hidden for people in their concrete experiences of life. Then God may be experienced as distant from a person or even as rejecting that person. But for Luther such trials of faith are necessary on the journey of faith, and will continue throughout one's whole life, and doubts and uncertainties are bound to occur. The only way out of trial is to turn to God, to argue with and complain to God, and to remind God of the promises given in God's word. In particular, a glance at Jesus Christ in his fear of death in Gethsemane (Mark 14:32–42), which was the great trial of the Son of God, will help a person not to lapse into despair. In Luther's understanding, trials are part of a living relationship with God, which cause people to argue with God and through this to intensify their relation to God.

Epilogue: Luther's Death

Martin Luther died on 18 February 1546 at the age of sixty-two. On 16 February he wrote the last of his extant written statements. In this, the last line reads:

We are beggars. That is true. (LW 54, 476)

This was the end of a short paragraph, which deals with the understanding of Scripture. Compared with the plenty which Holy Scripture contains, Luther considered that human beings are like beggars who may nevertheless hope to receive a portion of the fullness of life which Scripture speaks about.

In January 1546 Luther travelled to the small town of Eisleben for negotiations with the Counts of Mansfeld, to help them settle some problems in their family and in the organization of the town. He already had a presentiment of death. However, as he frequently did, he talked about the possibility of his own death with humour. On the journey he was accompanied by his three sons and his friend Justus Jonas. When they crossed the River Saale, which was dangerous because of high water, he said to Justus Jonas how enjoyable it would be for the devil if he, his sons and Jonas were to be drowned. However, he was only humorous about his own death – when others were dying he showed deep compassion and grief. He wept for a whole day following the death of a friend, and when his eight-month-old daughter Elisabeth died on 3 August 1528 he wrote in a letter:

> *My baby daughter, little Elisabeth, has passed away. It is amazing*
> *what a sick, almost woman-like heart she has left to me, so much has*
> *grief for her overcome me. Never before would I have believed that a*
> *father's heart could have such tender feelings for his child. Do pray to*
> *the Lord for me.* (LW 49, 203)

Despite all grief and even temptations to his faith through the
death of others, Luther believed that Jesus Christ once and for all
had broken the power of death. In a song he wrote:

> *That was a right wondrous strife*
> *When Death in Life's grip wallowed:*
> *Off victorious came Life,*
> *Death he has quite upswallowed ...*
> *Thus Death is become a laughter.*
> (HYMN, 'DEATH HELD OUR LORD IN PRISON', LW 53, 257)

Because of his belief in God having defeated death, Luther could
react to it with humour and with laughter though also with
anger. He knew its reality amidst human life, but he believed that
the Gospel of Jesus Christ had enabled Christians to say:

> *In the midst of death we are in Life's embraces.*

Even in the hour of his own death he believed he was held in the
embrace of the God of life. On 17 February his health fluctuated.
Before supper he complained about pains in the chest, which
faded when hot towels were applied. At supper he ate and drank
well; his conversation was as usual a mixture of humour and seri-
ousness. After his evening prayer Luther slept first on a sofa. He
awoke at a quarter past ten to go to bed. At one in the morning he
awoke, stood up and complained about a strong pain in the chest,
which presumably was caused by a heart attack. Doctors were
called, but Luther knew his end had come. He thanked God, and in

his fear comforted himself with words taken from the gospel of John and the psalms, particularly Psalm 68:20, 'To God, the Lord, belongs escape from death'. Then he prayed three times very quickly: 'Father, into thy hands I commit my spirit; thou hast redeemed me, O Lord, faithful God' (Luke 23:46 and Psalm 31:5). Thereafter he remained silent, and at a quarter to three in the morning, died.

Elector John Frederick of Sachsen insisted that Luther's remains were buried in Wittenberg. On 22 February interment took place near the pulpit of the Castle Church, where Luther's earthly remains have rested throughout the centuries.

Luther's ideas live on in the churches and the people he has inspired. It was Luther's unconditional commitment to the truth of the word of God which caused the Reformation. This commitment to truth should be at the centre of the life of all Christian churches, and this is the main heritage he has left to the world.

Suggested Further Reading

Luther's writings

Beside the large American edition of Luther's work with more than 50 volumes (see Abbreviations), there are smaller editions, which give a selection of his writings.

Brokering, H.F. (ed.), *Luther's Prayers*, Fortress Press, 1994.

Dillenberger, John (ed.), *Martin Luther, Selections from his Writings*, Doubleday, 1961.

Lull, Timothy F. (ed.), *Martin Luther's, Basic Theological Writings*, Fortress Press, 1989.

Pederson, Ph.E. (ed.), *What Does This Mean? Luther's Catechisms Today*, Augsburg Publishing House, 1979.

Porter, J. M. (ed.), *Martin Luther, Selected Political Writings*, University Press of America, 1988.

Rupp, E. B. and Drewery, B. (eds.), *Martin Luther*, Edward Arnold, London, 1970 (an anthology of Luther).

Russell, W. R. (ed.), *The Schmalkald Articles: Luther's Theological Testament*, Fortress Press, 1995.

Basic Luther. Four of His Fundamental Works, Templegate Publishers, 1994.

Martin Luther, The Bondage of the Will, James Clarke & Co., Cambridge, 1957 (and Revell Fleming, 1990).

Martin Luther, Table Talk, Fount, 1995. (A selection of recollections, by friends and family, of things Luther said informally. An easily

accessible and personal account of the German Reformation.)
Martin Luther, Three Treatises, Fortress Press, 1970. (Includes three of Luther's main writings of 1520: *To the Christian Nobility of the German Nation; The Babylonian Captivity of the Church; The Freedom of a Christian.*)

Writings about Luther's life and theology

Althaus, Paul, *The Theology of Martin Luther*, Fortress Press, 1966.

Atkinson, James, *Martin Luther and the Birth of Protestantism*, 1982.

Bainton, Roland H., *Here I Stand. A Life of Martin Luther*, Abingdon Press, 1978 (new edition: Lion Publishing, 1994).

Jüngel, Eberhard, *The Freedom of a Christian. Luther's Significance for Contemporary Theology*, Augsburg Publishing House, 1988.

Kittelson, James M., *Luther the Reformer*, Augsburg Publishing House, 1987.

Lindsay, Thomas Martin, *Martin Luther*, Christian Focus Publications, 1996.

Lohse, Bernhard, *Martin Luther. An Introduction to his Life and Work*, T. & T. Clark, Edinburgh, 1987.

McGrath, Alister E., *Luther's Theology of the Cross. Martin Luther's Theological Breakthrough*, Blackwell, Oxford, 1990.

Mullett, Michael A., *Luther*, Routledge, 1994.

Oberman, Heiko A., *Luther. Man between God and the Devil*, Fontana Press, 1993.

Rupp, Gordon, *Luther and Erasmus*, Westminster Press, 1978.

Smith, Preserved, *The Life and Letters of Martin Luther*, Hodder & Stoughton, London, 1993.

Books on the age of the Reformation

Oberman, Heiko A., *Dawn of the Reformation. Essays in Late Medieval and Early Reformation Thought*, T. & T. Clark, Edinburgh, 1992.

Ozment, Steven E., *The Age of Reform (1250–1550). An Intellectual and Religious History of Late Medieval and Reformation Europe*, Yale University Press, 1981.

Ozment, Steven E., *Protestants. The Birth of a Revolution*, Fontana Press, 1993.

Randell, Keith, *Luther and the German Reformation. 1517–55*, Hodder & Stoughton, 1989. (This was planned with the A-level student specifically in mind.)

Index

Adam's fall 23, 46, 80, 82, 86
Albert of Mainz (and Branden-
  burg) 6, 23, 25
amor sui 18
anabaptists 39–42
Aquinas, Thomas 6, 19
Aristotle 19, 21
Augustine 6, 16, 74, 80

baptism 23, 42
Barth, Karl 63
Bora, Katherine von 10, 82–3

Cajetan, Cardinal 6
calling 77–8
Calvin, Jean 62
Carlstadt, Andrew 40–41
catechism 44–5, 70
celibacy 79–81
Charles V, Emperor 1, 8, 9
church 39–40, 69–71
clarity of Scripture 43
commandments 15, 47–8
concupiscentia 18
condemnation 11, 15, 23
conscience 50–51

Counter-Reformation 11
crucifixion 86–8
culture 45

death 57, 63, 89, 93–5
despair 3, 29–31, 51, 87, 89
devil 51, 87, 89
Diet of Worms 7–8, 41, 50,
  73
doctrine of the two realms 75,
  77, 82

education 1, 78–9, 84
Erasmus of Rotterdam 9, 36,
  39, 43–4, 60–62, 74
eternal life 23–4
ethics 73–84
eucharist 9, 70–71
eunuchs 80
evil 17, 47, 65, 87–9
excommunication 7–8, 27–8,
  40

faith 26–7, 29, 33, 47, 55–7,
  73, 76
family 82, 84

family of Luther 1, 10, 93
Feuerbach, Ludwig 56
Frederick the Wise of Saxony 6–9
free will 43, 61, 74
freedom 44, 64, 73–5

German Bible 38
German language 7, 37
Gethsemane 91
glory 66, 68, 89
God 3, 5, 13, 33, 56–7
   God hidden 61–3, 87–8
   God revealed 62–3, 88
good works 76, 89
Gospel 15, 35, 37, 47–8, 52–3
grace of God 21, 31–3, 48, 52, 61
Gutenberg, Johann 35

heaven 25, 48
Heidelberg disputation 32, 86
hell 23, 25, 30, 48
Henry VIII of England 43
holiness 3, 48–9
Holy Scripture 11, 13, 29, 38–44, 88, 93
Holy Spirit 41–2
human nature 16–19, 74, 79
humanism 36–7
Hus, Jan 28

incarnation 86

individual 21, 26, 50, 57, 64, 69
indulgence 5, 23–9
inspiration 39
institutions 51, 82
intercession 67–8
interpretation of the Bible 5, 13, 35, 40, 42–4
invisible Church 70
Isaiah 48

Jesus Christ 31, 38–9, 43, 59–66, 85, 88, 94
Jonas, Justus 93
justice 20, 48
justification 20–21
justification by faith 33, 38, 76, 89
justification by works 32, 89

Kierkegaard, Søren 45, 88
kingdom of God 41
kingly office 67–8
knowledge of God 47, 60, 63–4, 85–6

law of God 35, 48–52
love 19, 33, 75–7, 79–80
love of God 20–21, 52, 60, 69

marriage 10, 79–84
married priests 40, 79
Melanchthon, Philipp 36, 37
merits of Christ 27
Michelangelo 1

Index

minister 42, 69–70
monks 2, 13, 77, 81
More, Thomas 36, 50
Müntzer, Thomas 41–2

New Testament 8, 23, 36–8
ninety-five theses 5, 23, 26

office of keys 24, 29, 32
Old Testament 37, 48

paradox 62–3, 88
parents 51, 84
peasants 9, 41
penance 23–4, 26, 32
philosophy 63–4
political use of the law 48–51
pope 3, 29, 32
Pope Leo X 6–7, 25, 27
prayer 68–9
predestination 61
priesthood of all believers 32,
    67–9
priestly office 67–8
priests 26, 29, 31, 67–9,
    77–8
projection 56
purgatory 23–5, 29

reality of God 56–7
reason 35, 44–7, 62, 82
rebellion against God 46, 55
Reformation 11, 23, 41, 75,
    95

remission of sins 31–2
Renaissance 1
repentance 26–7, 32–3
righteousness of God 3,
    13–15, 20
Rome 3, 6–7

sacraments 70, 82
salvation 29, 31, 33, 61,
    64–6
sciences 1, 45
self-authenticating of Scripture
    39
self-righteousness 47, 76
sexuality 79–84
sin 16–20, 32, 44, 48–9, 65,
    85
    actual sin 24
    original sin 23
society 48, 51, 78
St Anne 2
Staupitz, Johann 4, 63
St Peter 29, 32
St Peter's in Rome 25
suffering 60, 88–9
superbia 18

ten commandments 18, 49,
    51, 55
theologia crucis 86–9
theological use of the law of
    God 48
theology 32, 46, 63, 85–91
theology as science 90

theology of glory 87, 89
tower experience 13–15, 35
tradition 39
treasure of the Church 27
trial 63, 90–91
truth 11, 35, 39, 95

unfree will 19, 43, 61, 74
unity of the churches 70–71

virtues 13, 19, 45
visible churches 70

vocation 77–9
vow 2, 9, 13, 77, 81

Wartburg 8, 40
will of God 32, 60
wisdom 64
word of God 35, 38, 48, 73
worship 41, 70
wrath of God 30, 48

Zwingli, Huldrych 9